Lecture Notes
in Economics and
Mathematical Systems

Managing Editors: M. Beckmann and W. Krelle

237

Misspecification Analysis

Proceedings of a Workshop
Held in Groningen, The Netherlands
December 15–16, 1983

Edited by Theo K. Dijkstra

Springer-Verlag
Berlin Heidelberg New York Tokyo 1984

Managing Editors

Prof. Dr. M. Beckmann
Brown University
Providence, RI 02912, USA

Prof. Dr. W. Krelle
Institut für Gesellschafts- und Wirtschaftswissenschaften
der Universität Bonn
Adenauerallee 24–42, D-5300 Bonn, FRG

Editor

Dr. Theo K. Dijkstra
Institute of Econometrics, University of Groningen
WSN-Hoogbouw, P.O. Box 800, 9700 AV Groningen, The Netherlands

ISBN 3-540-13893-5 Springer-Verlag Berlin Heidelberg New York Tokyo
ISBN 0-387-13893-5 Springer-Verlag New York Heidelberg Berlin Tokyo

Printing and binding: Beltz Offsetdruck, Hemsbach/Bergstr.
2142/3140-543210

PREFACE

This volume collects papers prepared for the workshop "Misspecification Analysis" held in Groningen, The Netherlands, December 15th and 16th, 1983. The papers, which cover a wide range of problems, contain a number of interesting and fruitful ideas.

A bird's-eye view of the contents of the papers is as follows:

White describes in a very general setting properties of classical statistical procedures when models are misspecified.

Verbeek provides a lucid analysis of the statistical complexity of the model selection process.

Dijkstra indicates how to construct good estimators, taking the possibility of misspecification explicitly into account.

Taking the view that measured variables are never continuous, *De Leeuw* discusses in an illuminating way whether, and how, the discreteness of the data should and can be taken more seriously.

Starting from the thesis that models are at best useful approximations of reality, *Van Praag* and *Koster* derive properties of estimators determining best fitting hyperplanes.

Within the context of the errors-in-variables problem, *Bekker*, *Kapteyn* and *Wansbeek* provide an elegant description of the variation in estimation results due to part of the modelspecification varying, while estimators are adjusted so as to keep them consistent.

Bierens develops consistent tests of the hypothesis of parameter constancy against extremely diffuse alternatives.

It is well known that for prediction purposes it may pay to use fewer predictors than available. *Steerneman* introduces an interesting problem by showing that a classical predictor-selection procedure, put forward to optimize predictive quality, has many competitors with respect to asymptotic optimality.

The editor is grateful for helpful comments by D.A. Freedman (Berkeley), D.F. Hendry (Oxford), G.G. Judge (Illinois) and E.E. Leamer (UCLA). Financial support by the Netherlands organization for the advancement of pure research (Z.W.O.) is also gratefully acknowledged.

Theo K. Dijkstra.

TABLE OF CONTENTS

MAXIMUM LIKELIHOOD ESTIMATION OF MISSPECIFIED DYNAMIC MODELS

Halbert White
Department of Economics, D-008
University of California, San Diego
La Jolla, CA 92093

0. ABSTRACT

In this paper we present a number of results which describe the behavior of the maximum likelihood estimator of the parameters of a dynamic model which is incorrectly or incompletely specified. We provide conditions which ensure the existence of the Quasi-Maximum Likelihood Estimator (QMLE) and its consistency for the parameters of an approximation to the unknown true probability density which has optimal information theoretic properties. The ability of the QMLE to consistently estimate certain parameters of interest despite misspecification is investigated. We give conditions ensuring the asymptotic normality of the QMLE together with conditions under which its asymptotic covariance matrix may be consistently estimated. Two model specification tests are briefly discussed.

1. INTRODUCTION

Economic phenomena are so complex and the difficulties of measuring economic quantities are so formidable that it is difficult to believe that any mathematical model of a given economic phenomenon can ever be either a complete or accurate description of that phenomenon. At best, a parametric econometric model can be viewed as some kind of approximation to whatever the truth might be. But what kind of approximation? And what are the implications of estimating the parameters of such an approximation? How should they be interpreted? Can legitimate inferences be drawn regarding the relationships of interest, and if so, how? Are there ways to detect whether or not a particular approximation is exact, or perhaps only inaccurate in nonessential ways?

---

*The author is grateful for facilities provided by Australian National University and for financial support provided by NSF grant #SES-81-07552. I wish to thank Adrian Pagan, Peter Hall, Tony Hall, Des Nicholls, Mark Machina, Rob Engle, Herman Bierens, Theo Dijkstra, and participants of the UCSD Econometrics Workshop for their helpful comments. Any errors are the author's sole responsibility.

The results presented in this paper are designed to provide answers to these questions in a context which embraces a wide range of the kinds of phenomena and estimation techniques of interest to economists. Specifically, we consider maximum likelihood estimation of dynamic econometric models. The results are formulated in such a way as to apply to cross-sections also, as a special case. These results have been culled from the author's monograph on this subject (White [1984]). The reader is referred to the monograph for treatment of related issues, further heuristic development and discussion, more detailed discussion of the relation of these results to the current literature, and proofs of all results.

2. EXISTENCE AND CONSISTENCY

We suppose that we have data generated according to the following assumption.

ASSUMPTION 1: The observed data are a realization of a stochastic process $\{X_t: t = 1, 2, \ldots\}$ on a probability space $(\Omega, \mathcal{F}, P)$, where $\Omega = \times_{t=1}^{\infty} \mathbb{R}^v \equiv \mathbb{R}^v_\infty$ and $\mathcal{F}$ is the Borel σ-field generated by the measurable finite dimensional product cylinders.

The probability measure P provides a complete description of the relationships among the random $1 \times v$ vectors $X_1, X_2, \ldots$ which comprise our data. P is not assumed to be known, and our goal is to discover the relationships among our data by some suitable estimation technique. In what follows we partition X_t as $X_t = (Z_t, Y_t)$, where Z_t is $1 \times k$ and Y_t is $1 \times \ell$, so that $k+\ell = v$. This is convenient in cases where Y_t is a set of "dependent" variables to be determined (explained, forecasted) at least partly on the basis of "explanatory" variables Z_t.

A point ω in Ω can be viewed as representing the entire sequence $\{X_t\}$. We can regard X_t as the $\mathcal{F}$-measurable projection operator which selects ω_t, the tth coordinate of ω, so that $X_t(\omega) = \omega_t$. We also define $X^n = (X_1, \ldots, X_n)$ and $\omega^n = (\omega_1, \ldots, \omega_n)$ so that $X^n(\omega) = \omega^n$, a typical element of $\mathbb{R}^v_n = \times_{t=1}^{n} \mathbb{R}^v$.

The relationships among the data in a sample $X_1, \ldots, X_n$ are completely described by the finite dimensional distribution P_n defined as

$$P_n(B) \equiv P[(X_1, \ldots, X_n) \in B], \qquad B \in \mathcal{B}^v_n$$

where $\mathcal{B}^v_n$ is the Borel σ-field generated by the open sets of $\mathbb{R}^v_n$. The following assumption allows these relationships to be equivalently described by a joint density function.

ASSUMPTION 2: The probability measure $Q_{ti}(E) = P[X_{ti} \in E]$, $E \in \mathbb{B}$, where $\mathbb{B}$ is the Borel σ-field generated by the open sets of $\mathbb{R}$, is absolutely continuous with respect to a σ-finite measure ν_{ti} on $(\mathbb{R}, \mathbb{B})$, $t = 1, \ldots, n$, $i = 1, \ldots, v$.

This assumption essentially requires us to know whether our observed variables are continuous or discrete random variables, or some combination thereof. This is not a restrictive assumption. Together Assumptions 1 and 2 allow for the treatment of limited dependent variables and dummy explanatory variables as well as continuously distributed dependent or explanatory variables. As yet, P has not been restricted, so no conditions on the dependence or heterogeneity of the underlying stochastic process generating our data have yet been imposed. Mild restrictions will be added later.

To prove the existence of a joint density function for $X_1, \ldots, X_n$ we define the product measure μ_n on $(\mathbb{R}_n^v, \mathbb{B}_n^v)$ as

$$\mu_n \equiv \prod_{t=1}^{n} \nu_t \equiv \prod_{t=1}^{n} \prod_{i=1}^{v} \nu_{ti} \quad .$$

THEOREM 2.2: Given Assumptions 1 and 2, there exists a nonnegative $\mathbb{B}_n^v$-measurable density $g_n = dP_n/d\mu_n$ such that

$$P_n(B) = \int_B g_n \, d\mu_n$$

for all B in $\mathbb{B}_n^v$, $n = 1, 2, \ldots$. For two such densities g_n and f_n, $\mu_n(g_n \neq f_n) = 0$.

This establishes that the relationships among the data in our sample can be completely described by an appropriate joint density function g_n. Since P is unknown, P_n is unknown and therefore g_n is unknown. However, it may be possible to use the observed sample $(X_1, \ldots, X_n)$ to approximate g_n. This approximation may then be helpful in understanding the behavior of $\{X_t\}$ and the relationships among the elements of $\{X_t\}$.

Given a known approximation to g_n, say f_n, we can evaluate the adequacy of the approximation using the Kullback-Leibler Information Criterion (KLIC) (Kullback and Liebler [1951]).

THEOREM 2.3 (Information Inequality): Let f and g be nonnegative functions integrable with respect to a measure μ, and let $S = \{\omega: g(\omega) > 0\}$. Define the KLIC

$$\mathcal{I}(g:f) \equiv \int_S (\log g/f)\, g\, d\mu \ .$$

If $\int_S (g - f)\, d\mu \geq 0$, then $\mathcal{I}(g:f) \geq 0$, and $\mathcal{I}(g:f) = 0$ if and only if $g = f$ almost everywhere-μ.

Heuristically, the KLIC provides a precise information theoretic measure of the surprise we experience if we believe that a random phenomenon is described by the density f and it is then revealed to us that in fact the phenomenon is described by g. This surprise is always nonnegative and is zero if and only if our beliefs are essentially correct.

In approximating g_n, it is convenient to construct the approximation piece by piece, based upon a representation of g_n as a product of conditional densities. The approximation can then proceed by approximating each conditional density. For our purposes, it is convenient to consider the representation in terms of a conditional density of Y_t given Z_t and $X_1, \ldots, X_{t-1}$, and a conditional density of Z_t given $X_1, \ldots, X_{t-1}$. This is allowed by Theorem 2.4 below.

In order to state this result we introduce the following notation:

$$P'_t(B \times C) \equiv P[(X_1, \ldots, X_{t-1}) \in B,\ Z_t \in C] \qquad B \in \mathcal{B}^v_{t-1},\ C \in \mathcal{B}^k \ .$$

We define a corresponding measure $\mu'_t = \mu_{t-1} \nu^Z_t$, where $\nu^Z_t = \prod_{i=1}^k \nu_{ti}$. A result analogous to Theorem 2.2 holds for P'_t and μ'_t. We also define $Q^Y_t(D) \equiv P[Y_t \in D]$, $D \in \mathcal{B}^\ell$, $\nu^Y_t \equiv \prod_{i=k+1}^v \nu_{ti}$, and $Q^Z_t(C) = P[Z_t \in C]$, $C \in \mathcal{B}^k$.

The desired representation is given by the following result.

THEOREM 2.4: Given Assumptions 1 and 2

$$\log g_n(\omega^n) = \sum_{t=1}^n \log g^Y_t(\omega^t) + \log g^Z_t(\omega^{t-1}, z_t)$$

for all ω^n in $S_n = \{\omega^n : g_n(\omega^n) > 0\}$, where g^Y_t is a $\mathcal{B}^v_t$-measurable conditional density of Y_t given $X_1, \ldots, X_{t-1}, Z_t$ with respect to ν^Y_t, defined as

$$g^Y_t(\omega^t) \equiv g_t(\omega^t)/g'_t(\omega^{t-1}, z_t) \qquad g'_t(\omega^{t-1}, z_t) > 0$$

$$\equiv dQ^Y_t(y_t)/d\nu^Y_t(y_t) \qquad g'_t(\omega^{t-1}, z_t) = 0$$

with $g'_t(\omega^{t-1}, z_t)$ chosen as

$$g'_t(\omega^{t-1}, z_t) = \int_{\mathbb{R}^\ell} g_t(\omega^t)\, d\nu_t^Y(y_t) \qquad t = 1, \ldots, n;$$

and g_t^Z is a $\mathcal{B}_{t-1}^v \times \mathcal{B}^k$-measurable conditional density of Z_t given $X_1, \ldots, X_{t-1}$ with respect to ν_t^Z as

$$\begin{aligned} g_t^Z(\omega^{t-1}, z_t) &\equiv g'_t(\omega^{t-1}, z_t)/g_{t-1}(\omega^{t-1}) & g_{t-1}(\omega^{t-1}) > 0 \\ &\equiv dQ_t^Z(z_t)/d\nu_t^Z(z_t) & g_{t-1}(\omega^{t-1}) = 0 \end{aligned}$$

with $g_{t-1}(\omega^{t-1})$ chosen as

$$g_{t-1}(\omega^{t-1}) = \int_{\mathbb{R}^k} g'_t(\omega^{t-1}, z_t)\, d\nu_t^Z(z_t) \quad t = 2, \ldots, n .$$

For $t = 1$, set $g_t^Z(\omega^{t-1}, z_t) = dQ_1^Z(z_1)/d\nu_1^Z(z_1)$.

To make the conditional density representation more explicit, we shall write

$$g_t^Y(Y_t | \mathcal{F}'_{t-1}) = g_t^Y(\omega^t)$$

$$g_t^Z(Z_t | \mathcal{F}_{t-1}) = g_t^Z(\omega^{t-1}, z_t)$$

where $\mathcal{F}'_{t-1} = \sigma(X_1, \ldots, X_{t-1}, Z_t)$. This allows us to represent $\log g_n(\omega^n)$ as

$$\log g_n(\omega^n) = \sum_{t=1}^{n} \log g_t^Y(Y_t | \mathcal{F}'_{t-1}) + \log g_t^Z(Z_t | \mathcal{F}_{t-1}) \ .$$

A convenient method of approximating g_n is to specify a family of non-negative functions indexed by a parameter θ, say $f_n(\cdot, \theta)$, and then choose θ to maximize the likelihood function, defined below. We shall call $f_n(\cdot, \theta)$ the <u>specified model</u> for $(X_1, \ldots, X_n)$, or simply a <u>specification</u>. In economics, the specification of an approximation to g_t^Z is typically ignored, and an approximation to g_t^Y is typically based on only a subset of the information in $\mathcal{F}'_{t-1}$. Accordingly, we consider specifications based on the following assumption.

ASSUMPTION 3. The nonnegative functions $f_t^Y(Y_t | W_t; \theta) = f_t^Y(W_t(\omega), Y_t(\omega); \theta)$ are measurable-$\sigma(W_t, Y_t) \subset \mathcal{F}_t$ for each θ in Θ, a compact subset of $\mathbb{R}^p$, and continuous on Θ for each (w_t, y_t) uniformly in t, a.s.-P.

Note that the variables W_t are simply whatever variables the investigator has chosen for the purpose of explaining or forecasting Y_t. (W_t stands for "whatever.") They may include Z_t and any or all lagged values of $X_t = (Z_t, Y_t)$. Although the argument of f_t^Y has been written to suggest a conditional density, it does not even have to be a proper conditional density, and it may be different for each period t.

Given Assumption 3, we define the specification

$$f_n(\omega^n, \theta) = \prod_{t=1}^{n} f_t^Y(Y_t | W_t; \theta)$$

and the sample log-likelihood

$$\mathcal{L}_n(\omega^n, \theta) = n^{-1} \log f_n(\omega^n, \theta)$$

The value of θ which maximizes $\mathcal{L}_n$ will be called the Quasi-Maximum Likelihood Estimator (QMLE).

THEOREM 2.5 (Existence): Given Assumptions 1 and 3, for each n there exists a $\mathcal{B}_n^v$-measurable QMLE $\hat{\theta}_n(\omega^n)$ such that for all ω^n in $\mathbb{R}_n^v$

$$\mathcal{L}_n(\omega^n, \hat{\theta}_n(\omega^n)) = \max_{\theta \in \Theta} \mathcal{L}_n(\omega^n, \theta) .$$

This result says not only that there exists a value $\hat{\theta}_n$ which maximizes $\mathcal{L}_n$, but also that $\hat{\theta}_n$ is a random vector with stochastic properties which can be described completely on the basis of the underlying probability measure P_n (hence P). This is the meaning of the $\mathcal{B}_n^v$-measurability of $\hat{\theta}_n$.

We investigate the stochastic behavior of $\hat{\theta}_n$ in large samples. This behavior is suggested by the heuristic idea that since $\hat{\theta}_n$ maximizes $\mathcal{L}_n(\omega^n, \theta)$ and since the law of large numbers should ensure that $\mathcal{L}_n(\omega^n, \theta)$ will generally tend to $\bar{\mathcal{L}}_n(\theta) \equiv E(\mathcal{L}_n(\omega^n, \theta))$, then $\hat{\theta}_n$ should tend to that value of θ, say θ_n^*, which maximizes $\bar{\mathcal{L}}_n(\theta)$. To ensure the validity of this intuition (which requires the validity of a law of large numbers) we now impose additional structure on the probability measure and on the specification f_t^Y.

For two σ-fields $\mathcal{G}$ and $\mathcal{H}$, define

$$\phi(\mathcal{G}, \mathcal{H}) \equiv \sup_{\{G \in \mathcal{G},\ H \in \mathcal{H}:\ P(G) > 0\}} |P(H|G) - P(H)|$$

$$\alpha(\mathcal{G}, \mathcal{H}) \equiv \sup_{\{G \in \mathcal{G},\ H \in \mathcal{H}\}} |P(H \cap G) - P(H)P(G)| \quad .$$

Let $\mathcal{F}^{t}_{-\infty} = \sigma(\ldots X_t)$ and let $\mathcal{F}^{\infty}_{t+m} = \sigma(X_{t+m}, \ldots)$. A measure of the dependence between events separated by at least m time periods is given by either

$$\phi(m) = \sup_t \phi(\mathcal{F}^{t}_{-\infty}, \mathcal{F}^{\infty}_{t+m})$$

$$\alpha(m) = \sup_t \alpha(\mathcal{F}^{t}_{-\infty}, \mathcal{F}^{\infty}_{t+m})$$

If $\phi(m) = 0$ or $\alpha(m) = 0$ for all $m \geq 1$, then $\{X_t\}$ is an independent sequence, while if $\phi(m) = 0$ or $\alpha(m) = 0$ for all $m > q$, then $\{X_t\}$ is a q-dependent sequence. If $\phi(m)$ or $\alpha(m)$ tend to zero as $m \to \infty$ then $\{X_t\}$ can be thought of as possessing an "asymptotic independence" property in the sense that events occurring now are almost independent of events which occurred in the far distant past.

We shall require that $\phi(m)$ or $\alpha(m)$ approach zero at a specific rate. If a is a positive real number and if $\phi(m) = O(m^{-\lambda})$ for $\lambda > a$, we say that $\phi(m)$ <u>is of size</u> a. Similarly, if $\alpha(m) = O(m^{-\lambda})$ for $\lambda > a$, we say that $\alpha(m)$ <u>is of size</u> a. Such conditions are called mixing conditions. They are not very restrictive and are plausibly applied to economic data.

We impose the mixing conditions by strengthening Assumption 1.

ASSUMPTION 1′: Assumption 1 holds, and $\{X_t\}$ has either $\phi(m)$ of size $r/(2r-1)$, $r \geq 1$ or $\alpha(m)$ of size $r/(r-1)$, $r > 1$.

To ensure that $f^Y_t(Y_t|W_t;\theta)$ is a mixing sequence, we strengthen Assumption 3 as follows.

ASSUMPTION 3′: Assumption 3 holds with $\sigma(W_t, Y_t) \subset \mathcal{F}^{t}_{t-\tau} \equiv \sigma(X_{t-\tau}, \ldots, X_t)$, $\tau < \infty$, $t = 1, 2, \ldots$.

This says that the specified model explicitly includes only a finite number of lagged values of X_t. This assumption can be relaxed substantially. We impose it for convenience, since without further technical assumptions, functions of infinite lags of mixing processes are not necessarily mixing.

To apply a uniform law of large numbers we impose the following domination condition.

ASSUMPTION 4: For all θ in Θ $|\log f_t^Y(Y_t|W_t; \theta)| < d_t(W_t, Y_t)$ where $E|d_t(W_t, Y_t)|^{r+\delta} < \Delta < \infty$ for some $\delta > 0$, $t = 1, 2, \ldots$.

When Assumption 4 holds, we say that $\log f_t^Y$ is "dominated in absolute value by uniformly $r+\delta$ integrable functions." This assumption imposes mild restrictions on the allowable heterogeneity exhibited by the data, and can be thought of as analogous to the imposition of moment restrictions on the regressors in a linear regression model. (E.g., that such regressors have uniformly bounded $2+\delta$ moments.)

To ensure that $\hat{\theta}_n$ tends to a unique limit, we impose an identification condition based on the following definition of Domowitz and White [1982].

DEFINITION 2.6: Let $\bar{Q}_n(\theta)$ be a real valued function continuous on a compact set Θ such that $\bar{Q}_n(\theta)$ has a maximum at θ_n^*, $n = 1, 2, \ldots$. Let $\mathcal{S}_n(\varepsilon)$ be an open sphere centered at θ_n^* with fixed radius $\varepsilon > 0$. For each $n = 1, 2, \ldots$ define the neighborhood $\eta_n(\varepsilon) = \mathcal{S}_n(\varepsilon) \cap \Theta$ with compact complement $\eta_n^c(\varepsilon)$ in Θ. The sequence of maximizers $\{\theta_n^*\}$ is said to be <u>identifiably unique</u> if and only if

$$\limsup_n \left[\max_{\theta \in \eta_n^c(\varepsilon)} \bar{Q}_n(\theta) - \bar{Q}_n(\theta_n^*) \right] < 0$$

for any $\varepsilon > 0$.

ASSUMPTION 5: The sequence $\{\bar{\mathcal{L}}_n(\theta)\}$ has identifiably unique maximizers $\{\theta_n^*\}$.

This condition ensures that $\bar{\mathcal{L}}_n$ does not become increasingly flat in the neighborhood of θ_n^*. In a linear regression model this assumption rules out multicolinearity for sufficiently large samples.

The limiting behavior of $\hat{\theta}_n$ is given by the following result.

THEOREM 2.7 (Consistency): Suppose Assumptions 1′, 3′, 4 and 5 hold and that $\hat{\theta}_n$ is the QMLE. Then $\hat{\theta}_n - \theta_n^* \xrightarrow{a.s.} 0$.

In order to give θ_n^* an information theoretic interpretation, we impose assumptions which ensure that the information inequality can be applied in a manner consistent with the present context. Since f_t^Y pays no attention to the approximation of the density g_t^Z, it can happen that

$$\mathcal{I}(g_n : f_n; \theta) \equiv \int_{S_n} [\log g_n(\omega^n)/f_n(\omega^n, \theta)]\, g_n(\omega^n)\, d\mu_n(\omega^n)$$

can assume negative values. To avoid this difficulty, we consider

$$\mathcal{I}(g_t^Y : f_t^Y ; \theta) \equiv \int_{S_t^Y} [\log g_t^Y(\omega^t)/f_t^Y(w_t, y_t; \theta)]\, g_t^Y(\omega^t)\, d\nu_t^Y(y_t)$$

where $S_t^Y = \{y_t : g_t^Y(\omega^t) > 0\}$, and define

$$\bar{\mathcal{I}}_n(\{g_t^Y : f_t^Y\}; \theta) \equiv n^{-1} \sum_{t=1}^{n} E(\mathcal{I}(g_t^Y : f_t^Y ; \theta)) \quad .$$

The function $\bar{\mathcal{I}}_n$ can be interpreted as the average expected surprise experienced when we believe that the conditional density of Y_t given Z_t and $X_{t-1}, \ldots, X_1$ is given by $f_t^Y(Y_t | W_t; \theta)$ and it is then revealed that in fact the conditional density is $g_t^Y(\omega^t)$.

We now require that f_t^Y be a conditional density function, or more generally, a "subdensity."

ASSUMPTION 6: For all θ in Θ, $\int_{\mathbb{R}^\ell} f_t^Y(w_t, y_t; \theta)\, d\nu_t^Y(y_t) \le 1$, $t = 1, 2, \ldots$.

We call f_t^Y a "subdensity" since it may integrate to a value less than one. This value may depend on θ. Assumption 6 will be satisfied, however, whenever f_t^Y is a proper conditional density.

To ensure that $\bar{\mathcal{I}}_n$ is not infinite for all values of θ we impose the following condition.

ASSUMPTION 7: $\log g_t^Y(\omega^t)$ is integrable, uniformly in t.

With the addition of Assumptions 6 and 7, we can give θ_n^* the following interpretation in terms of $\bar{\mathcal{I}}_n$.

THEOREM 2.8: Given Assumptions 1-3, 5, 6 and 7, θ_n^* is the identifiably unique minimizer of $\bar{\mathcal{I}}_n(\{g_t^Y : f_t^Y\}; \theta) \ge 0$.

In other words, $\hat{\theta}_n$ provides a consistent estimator for the parameter vector θ_n^* which minimizes our ignorance (the average expected surprise) regarding the true conditional density of Y_t given $X_1, \ldots, X_{t-1}, Z_t$.

Given the generality of our assumptions, this result can be understood as holding for most of the kinds of data (time-series, cross-section, or panel data), for most of the kinds of models (single equation, simultaneous equation, logit, probit, tobit, hazard rate, poisson, etc.), and for many of the kinds of estimators (any maximum likelihood-like or asymptotically equivalent procedure, including two-step and many instrumental variables procedures) of interest to economists.

When the model is correctly specified in the sense that $f_t^Y(Y_t|W_t;\theta)$ equals the true conditional density of Y_t given W_t for some parameter values θ_o, it turns out that $\theta_n^* = \theta_o$. The assumption of a correctly specified model is formally stated as follows.

ASSUMPTION 8: There exists θ_o in Θ such that $g_t^Y(Y_t|W_t) = f_t^Y(w_t, y_t; \theta_o)$ a.e.-$\nu_t^Y \nu_t^W$, where

$$\nu_t^W = (\Pi_{\tau=1}^{t-1} \Pi_{i=1}^{v} \nu_{\tau i}{}^1[\omega_{\tau i} \in w_t]) \Pi_{i=1}^{k} \nu_{ti}{}^1[\omega_{ti} \in w_t] .$$

In this assumption ν_t^W is simply the product measure corresponding to W_t. Note that we assume only that f_t^Y is correctly specified for $g_t^Y(Y_t|W_t)$. It may or may not be true that $g_t^Y(Y_t|W_t) = g_t^Y(Y_t|\mathfrak{F}_t')$. If not, a form of dynamic misspecification is still present. Despite this, $\hat{\theta}_n$ is still a consistent estimator for θ_o, as a consequence of the following result.

COROLLARY 2.9: Given Assumptions 1-8, $\theta_n^* = \theta_o$.

This implies that if the model specified is a correctly specified version of the conditional density of Y_t given <u>any</u> specific set of conditioning variables, then the QMLE provides consistent estimates of the "true" parameters of that conditional density. For example, OLS applied to a linear regression with serially correlated errors provides consistent estimates of the regression parameters when no lagged dependent variables are present. Similarly, application of the Tobit method yields consistent parameter estimates in the presence of normally distributed serial correlated errors (see Robinson [1982]). The same result holds for Probit models. Of course, Corollary 2.9 also applies when there is no dynamic misspecification, and so guarantees the consistency of the MLE for vector autoregression models. Corollary 2.9 was first given by Levine [1983] under slightly stronger conditions.

Taken together, Theorems 2.7 and 2.8 and Corollary 2.9 generalize results of White [1982], Vuong [1983], Anderson [1971] and Levine [1983] for maximum likelihood estimation of correctly or incorrectly specified conditional or unconditional models.

Often interest attaches only to consistent estimation of the parameters of the conditional mean. Gourieroux, Monfort and Trognon [1984] (GMT) have shown that if the model specified is a member of the linear exponential family then the

QMLE yields consistent estimates of the parameters of the conditional mean regardless of whether or not the true data generation process is a member of the linear exponential family. Their results are obtained for models without dynamics and with i.i.d. errors, but their results extend directly to the present context. The linear exponential specification is imposed as follows.

ASSUMPTION 9: (a) For all θ in Θ, the closure of an open connected set, and for some σ-finite measure η_t the model specified satisfies

$$\int_{\mathbb{R}^\ell} f_t^Y(w_t, y_t; \theta)\, d\eta_t(y_t) = 1$$

$$m_t(w_t, \theta) = \int_{\mathbb{R}^\ell} y_t f_t^Y(w_t, y_t; \theta)\, d\eta_t(y_t) \qquad t = 1, 2, \ldots \quad .$$

(b) The model is specified as

$$\log f_t^Y(Y_t | W_t; \theta) = A_t(m_t(W_t, \theta)) + B_t(Y_t) + Y_t C_t(m_t(W_t, \theta)) \qquad t = 1, 2, \ldots$$

where $m_t(w_t, \theta) \in \mathcal{M}_t \subset \mathbb{R}^\ell$ for all θ in Θ and w_t, $A_t\colon \mathbb{R}^\ell \to \mathbb{R}^1$, $B_t\colon \mathbb{R}^\ell \to \mathbb{R}^1$ and $C_t\colon \mathbb{R}^\ell \to \mathbb{R}^\ell$.

Taken together Assumptions 9(a) and 9(b) imply that $\mu \nabla C_t(\mu) = -\nabla A_t(\mu)$. As special cases, Assumption 9 includes the Bernoulli, binomial, Poisson, negative binomial, hypergeometric, and logarithmic series densities and their multivariate generalizations (e.g. Johnson and Kotz [1969]) such as the multinomial and negative multinomial, as well as the normal, gamma (including χ^2), Pareto, and Weibull distributions. In each of the cases mentioned, there may be some parameters which must be assumed "known."

The assumption that the conditional mean is correctly specified is now given.

ASSUMPTION 10: For some θ_o in Θ, $E(Y_t | W_t) = m_t(W_t, \theta_o)$, $t = 1, 2, \ldots$.

The GMT result extends in the following way to the present context.

THEOREM 2.10: (a) Given Assumptions 1′, 3′, 4, 5 and 9, $\hat{\theta}_n - \theta_n^* \xrightarrow{a.s.} 0$, where θ_n^* is the identifiably unique maximizer of

$$n^{-1} \sum_{t=1}^{n} E(A_t[m_t(W_t, \theta)] + Y_t C_t[m_t(W_t, \theta)])$$

$$= n^{-1} \sum_{t=1}^{n} E(A_t[m_t(W_t, \theta)] + E(Y_t | W_t) C_t[m_t(W_t, \theta)])$$

where the equality holds provided $E(Y_t) < \infty$. (b) If Assumption 10 also holds, then $\theta_n^* = \theta_o$.

For example, consider the special case of the multivariate normal density, for which

$$A_t(\mu) = -\mu\mu'/2$$

$$B_t(Y_t) = -(Y_t Y_t' + \log 2\pi + 1)/2$$

$$C_t(\mu) = \mu .$$

Expression formally, we have

ASSUMPTION 11: The model is specified as

$$\log f_t^Y(Y_t | W_t; \theta) = -\frac{1}{2}\ell \cdot \log 2\pi - \frac{1}{2}\log |I_\ell|$$

$$- \frac{1}{2}(Y_t - m_t(W_t, \theta))(Y_t - m_t(W_t, \theta))' .$$

COROLLARY 2.11: (a) Given Assumptions 1′, 3′, 4, 5 and 11, $\hat{\theta}_n - \theta_n^* \xrightarrow{a.s.} 0$, where θ_n^* minimizes

$$n^{-1} \sum_{t=1}^{n} \operatorname{tr} E([Y_t - m_t(W_t, \theta)]'[Y_t - m_t(W_t, \theta)]) ,$$

the average value of the trace of the mean squared error matrix for $m_t(W_t, \theta)$ as a predictor of Y_t. Furthermore, if $E(Y_t) < \infty$, θ_n^* minimizes

$$n^{-1} \sum_{t=1}^{n} \operatorname{tr} E([E(Y_t | W_t) - m_t(W_t, \theta)]'[E(Y_t | W_t) - m_t(W_t, \theta)]) .$$

(b) If Assumption 10 also holds, then $\theta_n^* = \theta_o$.

This result applies to most least squares based estimation procedures for single equations or systems of equations with or without linear or nonlinear cross-equation restrictions such as those arising from overidentifying structural restrictions or from rational expectation models. Least squares estimation of misspecified dynamic models is extensively discussed by Domowitz and White [1982].

GMT also establish a converse to their version of Theorem 2.10, which says essentially that the linear exponential family is the only family with the property that $\theta_n^* = \theta_o$ regardless of the true data generating process when the conditional mean is correctly specified. To establish a converse to Theorem 2.10, we add some further assumptions which allow us to make use of the first order conditions for the QMLE.

ASSUMPTION 12: For each ω in Ω, f_t^Y is continuously differentiable on Θ uniformly in t, a.s.-P.

ASSUMPTION 5′: Assumption 5 holds and θ_n^* is interior to Θ, uniformly in n.

A precise statement of the converse to Theorem 2.10 is

THEOREM 2.12: Given Assumptions 3, 9(a) and 12, suppose that $\theta_n^* = \theta_o$, $n = 1, 2, \ldots$ for any probability measure P such that Assumptions 1, 4, 5′ and 10 are satisfied. Then Assumption 9(b) holds, i.e. f_t^Y is a member of the linear exponential family for $t = 1, 2, \ldots$.

3. ASYMPTOTIC NORMALITY

In this section, we introduce additional conditions which ensure the asymptotic normality of the QMLE. Asymptotic normality is established by taking a mean-value expansion of the first order conditions for a maximum of the sample log-likelihood function. To allow this we assume that f_t^Y is appropriately differentiable.

ASSUMPTION 12′: For each ω in Ω, f_t^Y is continuously differentiable of order 2 on Θ uniformly in t a.s.-P.

The mean value expansion allows us to write

$$\sqrt{n}(\hat{\theta}_n - \theta_n^*) = -\bar{H}_n^{-1}\, n^{-1/2} \sum_{t=1}^{n} \nabla \log f_t^Y(Y_t | W_t ; \theta_n^*)$$

where $\bar{H}_n$ is the hessian of the sample log-likelihood function with rows evaluated at suitable mean values and ∇ is the gradient operator with respect to θ. The asymptotic normality result follows provided that $\bar{H}_n$ tends to an appropriate limit and that the summation above (the "score") obeys a central limit theorem. The following assumption imposes domination conditions which help ensure these properties.

ASSUMPTION 4′: (i) Assumption 4 holds; (ii) $\{(\nabla \log f_t^Y)' \nabla \log f_t^Y\}$ is dominated by uniformly r′-integrable functions, $r' > 1$; and (iii) $\{\nabla^2 \log f_t^Y\}$ is dominated in absolute value by uniformly $r+\delta$-integrable functions, $r \geq 1$, $\delta > 0$.

We apply a central limit theorem for mixing processes to the score by defining

$$I_{a,n}(\theta) \equiv \text{var}\left(n^{-1/2} \sum_{t=a+1}^{a+n} \nabla \log f_t^Y(Y_t | W_t; \theta)\right)$$

$$I_{a,n}^* \equiv I_{a,n}(\theta_n^*)$$

This is the variance-covariance matrix of the score for a sample of size n beginning in time period $a+1$. For $a = 0$, we define

$$I_n^* \equiv I_{o,n}^* \quad .$$

This is the information matrix. The central limit theorem used to establish asymptotic normality of the score makes use of the following asymptotic covariance stationarity assumption.

ASSUMPTION 13: There exists a symmetric positive definite matrix I such that $\lambda' I_{a,n}^* \lambda - \lambda' I \lambda \to 0$ as $n \to \infty$ uniformly in a for any real nonzero $p \times 1$ vector λ.

To ensure that $\bar{H}_n$ converges to a nonsingular limit, we define

$$H_n(\theta) \equiv E\left(n^{-1} \sum_{t=1}^{n} \nabla^2 \log f_t^Y(Y_t | W_t; \theta)\right)$$

$$H_n^* \equiv H_n(\theta_n^*) \quad ,$$

and impose

ASSUMPTION 14: The matrix $H_n(\theta)$ has constant rank in some open ε-neighborhood of θ_n^* for all n sufficiently large, uniformly in n.

We also strengthen the mixing conditions to allow application of an appropriate central limit theorem.

ASSUMPTION 1″: Assumption 1 holds and $\{X_t\}$ has either $\phi(m)$ or $\alpha(m)$ of size $r'/(r'-1)$, where $r' = r + \delta$.

THEOREM 3.1 (Asymptotic Normality): Given Assumptions 1″, 3′, 4′, 5′, 12′, 13 and 14, $\sqrt{n}\, I_n^{*-1/2} H_n^*(\hat{\theta}_n - \theta_n^*) \overset{A}{\sim} N(0, I)$.

Under general conditions, then, the QMLE is distributed approximately as normal in large samples, with covariance matrix $H_n^{*-1} I_n^* H_n^{*-1}$. This property can be exploited to test hypotheses about θ_n^* using Wald or Lagrange multiplier tests similar to those given by White [1982], provided that a consistent estimator for $H_n^{*-1} I_n^* H_n^{*-1}$ is available.

It is straightforward to show that

$$\hat{H}_n \equiv n^{-1} \sum_{t=1}^{n} \nabla^2 \log f_t^Y(Y_t | W_t; \hat{\theta}_n)$$

is a consistent estimator for H_n^*. Estimating I_n^* is somewhat more difficult, and results for the general QMLE are not yet available. However, recent results of White and Domowitz [1984] suggest that a consistent estimator can be obtained for linear exponential specifications of the following form.

ASSUMPTION 15: $\nabla \log f_t^Y(Y_t | W_t; \theta)$ has the form

$$\nabla \log f_t^Y(Y_t | W_t; \theta) = a(\theta) + b(Y_t, W_t) + \sum_{k=1}^{K} c_{tk}(Y_t, W_t) d_k(\theta) \quad .$$

The estimator is motivated by the fact that

$$\begin{aligned} \bar{I}_n \equiv\ & n^{-1} \sum_{t=1}^{n} E(\nabla \log f_t^Y(Y_t | W_t; \theta_n^*)\ \nabla \log f_t^Y(Y_t | W_t; \theta_n^*)') \\ & + n^{-1} \sum_{\tau=1}^{\ell} \sum_{t=\tau+1}^{n} E[\nabla \log f_t^Y(Y_t | W_t; \theta_n^*)\ \nabla \log f_{t-\tau}^Y(Y_{t-\tau} | W_{t-\tau}; \theta_n^*)' \\ & + \nabla \log f_{t-\tau}^Y(Y_{t-\tau} | W_{t-\tau}; \theta_n^*)\ \nabla \log f_t^Y(Y_t | W_t; \theta_n^*)'] \end{aligned}$$

should provide a useful approximation to

$$\ddot{I}_n \equiv I_n^* + n^{-1} \sum_{t=1}^{n} \sum_{\tau=1}^{n} E(\nabla \log f_t^Y(Y_t | W_t; \theta_n^*))\ E(\nabla \log f_\tau^Y(Y_\tau | W_\tau; \theta_n^*)')$$

as long as ℓ tends to ∞ in an appropriate way as $n \to \infty$. (Note that $\bar{I}_n = \ddot{I}_n$ if

$\ell = n-1$ and $I_n^* = \ddot{I}_n$ when the double summation vanishes.) This occurs because the mixing conditions ensure that terms in $\ddot{I}_n$ neglected by $\bar{I}_n$ when $\ell < n-1$ will be small. In turn, the matrix $\bar{I}_n$ may be usefully estimated by

$$\hat{I}_n \equiv n^{-1} \sum_{t=1}^{n} \nabla \log f_t^Y(Y_t | W_t; \hat{\theta}_n) \nabla \log f_t^Y(Y_t | W_t; \hat{\theta}_n)'$$

$$+ n^{-1} \sum_{\tau=1}^{\ell} \sum_{t=\tau+1}^{n} [\nabla \log f_t^Y(Y_t | W_t; \hat{\theta}_n) \nabla \log f_{t-\tau}^Y(Y_{t-\tau} | W_{t-\tau}; \hat{\theta}_n)'$$

$$+ \nabla \log f_{t-\tau}^Y(Y_{t-\tau} | W_{t-\tau}; \hat{\theta}_n) \nabla \log f_t^Y(Y_t | W_t; \hat{\theta}_n)']$$

To show the consistency of $\hat{I}_n$ for $\bar{I}_n$ we strengthen the domination and mixing conditions as follows.

ASSUMPTION 16: $\{[(\nabla \log f_t^Y)' \nabla \log f_t^Y]^2\}$ is dominated by uniformly $r+\delta$-integrable functions, $r \geq 1$, $\delta > 0$.

ASSUMPTION 1‴: Assumption 1 holds and $\{X_t\}$ has either $\phi(m)$ of size 2 or $\alpha(m)$ of size $2r'/(r'-1)$, $r' > 1$.

THEOREM 3.2: Given Assumptions 1‴, 3′, 4′, 5′, 12′, and 13-16, if $\ell \to \infty$ as $n \to \infty$ such that $\ell = o(n^{1/3})$ then $\hat{I}_n - \bar{I}_n \xrightarrow{p} 0$.

In other words, as long as $\ell \to \infty$ as $n \to \infty$, but more slowly than $n^{1/3}$, $\hat{I}_n$ is a consistent estimator for $\bar{I}_n$. Whether $\hat{I}_n$ is consistent for I_n^* depends upon whether $\bar{I}_n$ converges to I_n^*. This is not guaranteed in the present context since $\ddot{I}_n$ need not equal I_n^*. This is due to the presence of the double summation term in the equation defining $\ddot{I}_n$, which vanishes when there is no dynamic misspecification or when the $\{X_t\}$ process is stationary. The next result gives a necessary and sufficient condition for $\bar{I}_n$ to tend to I_n^*.

THEOREM 3.3: Given Assumptions 1‴, 3′, 4′, 5′, 12′ and 13-16, $\bar{I}_n - I_n^* \to 0$ as $n \to \infty$ if and only if

$$n^{-1} \sum_{\tau=\ell+1}^{n-1} \sum_{t=\tau+1}^{n} E(\nabla \log f_t^Y(Y_t | W_t; \theta_n^*)) E(\nabla \log f_{t-\tau}^Y(Y_{t-\tau} | W_{t-\tau}; \theta_n^*)') \to 0$$

as $n \to \infty$.

If this condition fails (as it generally will when the model exhibits dynamic misspecification and the data are not generated by a stationary process) then it is not possible to find a consistent estimator for the asymptotic covariance matrix of $\hat{\theta}_n$, or even to provide appropriate bounds. Otherwise, a consistent estimator is available, as stated by the following theorem.

COROLLARY 3.4: Given Assumptions 1‴, 3′, 4′, 5′, 12′, 13-16 and the condition of Theorem 3.3, then

$$\hat{H}_n^{-1} \hat{I}_n \hat{H}_n^{-1} - H_n^{*-1} I_n^{*} H_n^{*-1} \xrightarrow{p} 0 .$$

White [1982] gives sufficient conditions for the information matrix equality, i.e. $H_n^* = - I_n^*$, for the case of i.i.d. observations. We can extend those results to the present context as follows. Define

$$H_n^o \equiv H_n(\theta_o)$$

$$I_n^o \equiv E\left(n^{-1} \sum_{t=1}^{n} \nabla \log f_t^Y(Y_t | W_t; \theta_o) \nabla \log f_t^Y(Y_t | W_t; \theta_o)'\right)$$

We require that f_t^Y be a conditional density, for all θ in Θ.

ASSUMPTION 6′: For all θ in Θ, $\int_{\mathbb{R}^\ell} f_t^Y(w_t, y_t; \theta) d\nu_t^Y(y_t) = 1$, $t = 1, 2, \ldots$.

To allow differentiation to be taken inside the integral in Assumption 6′, we impose the following two assumptions.

ASSUMPTION 17: (i) $f_t^Y(Y_t | W_t; \theta)$ is dominated by a function integrable with respect to $\nu_t^Y P_t'$, $t = 1, \ldots, n$; (ii) the elements of $\nabla \log f_t^Y(Y_t | W_t; \theta) \nabla \log f_t^Y(Y_t | W_t; \theta)'$ are dominated by functions integrable with respect to $\nu_t^Y P_t'$, $t = 1, \ldots, n$.

ASSUMPTION 18: The support of f_t^Y does not depend on θ.

THEOREM 3.5: Given Assumptions 1-3, 12′, 16-18 and Assumption 8, i.e. f_t^Y is a correctly specified model of the conditional density of Y_t given W_t, then

$$H_n^o = - I_n^o .$$

Note that I_n^o is only one term of the full expression for I_n^*. For the information matrix equivalence to hold in its entirety it suffices that there is no dynamic misspecification.

THEOREM 3.6: Given Assumptions 1-3, 12′, 16-18, 8 and if $g_t^Y(Y_t|W_t) = g_t^Y(Y_t|\mathfrak{F}'_{t-1})$, then

$$H_n^o = -I_n^o = -I_n^* .$$

4. SPECIFICATION TESTS

The results of Sections 2 and 3 suggest a variety of testing procedures which may be useful in testing the correctness of a particular specification, as expressed by Assumption 8 or 10. Here we briefly discuss two procedures suggested by Theorems 3.5 and 3.6.

In particular, Theorem 3.5 suggests that the validity of Assumption 8 can be investigated by comparing an estimator of H_n^o to an estimator of I_n^o. A statistic designed to test the hypothesis that $H_n^o = -I_n^o$ can be obtained as n times the R^2 of the regression of a constant equal to unity on a vector of regressors containing $\nabla \log f_t^Y(Y_t|W_t;\hat{\theta}_n)$ and q nonredundant elements of

$$\nabla^2 \log f_t^Y(Y_t|W_t;\hat{\theta}_n) - \nabla \log f_t^Y(Y_t|W_t;\hat{\theta}_n)\nabla \log f_t^Y(Y_t|W_t;\hat{\theta}_n)'$$

where $q \le p(p+1)/2$. Which elements are selected will determine the particular alternatives against which the test will have power. Under general conditions, this statistic (nR^2) will have the χ_q^2 distribution asymptotically when Assumption 8 holds and $g_t^Y(Y_t|\mathfrak{F}'_{t-1}) = g_t^Y(Y_t|W_t)$.

The hypothesis that $I_n^o = I_n^*$ can be tested by estimating the coefficients of the vector autoregression

$$\nabla \log f_t^Y(Y_t|W_t;\hat{\theta}_n) = R_1 \nabla \log f_{t-1}(Y_{t-1}|W_{t-1};\hat{\theta}_n) + \ldots$$

$$+ R_\tau \nabla \log f_{t-\tau}^Y(Y_{t-\tau}|W_{t-\tau};\hat{\theta}_n)$$

and then testing the hypothesis that $R_1 = \ldots = R_\tau = 0$, where τ is a fixed prespecified integer. When Assumption 8 holds and $g_t^Y(Y_t|\mathfrak{F}'_{t-1}) = g_t^Y(Y_t|W_t)$, the appropriate Wald or Lagrange multiplier statistics will have the $\chi^2_{\tau p^2}$ distribution asymptotically, under general conditions.

REFERENCES

Andersen, E. B. [1970], "Asymptotic Properties of Conditional Maximum Likelihood Estimators," Journal of the Royal Statistical Society, Series B, 32, 283-301.

Domowitz, I. and White, H. [1982], "Misspecified Models with Dependent Observations," Journal of Econometrics: Annals, 20, 35-58.

Gourieroux, C., Monfort, A. and Trognon, A. [1984], "Pseudo Maximum Likelihood Methods: Theory," Econometrica, 52, forthcoming.

Johnson, N. L. and Kotz, S. [1972], Distributions in Statistics: Discrete Distributions, Boston: Houghton Miflin Co.

Kullback, S. and Leibler, R. A. [1951], "On Information and Sufficiency," Annals of Mathematical Statistics, 22, 79-86.

Levine, D. [1983], "A Remark on Serial Correlation in Maximum Likelihood," Journal of Econometrics, 23, 337-342.

Robinson, P. [1982], "On the Asymptotic Properties of Estimators of Models Containing Limited Dependent Variables," Econometrica, 50, 27-42.

Vuong, C. H. [1983], "Misspecification and Conditional Maximum Likelihood Estimation," California Institute of Technology Working Paper.

White, H. [1982], "Maximum Likelihood Estimation of Misspecified Models," Econometrica, 50, 1-26.

White, H. [1984], Estimation, Inference and Specification Analysis, New York: Cambridge University Press, forthcoming.

White, H. and Domowitz, I. [1984], "Nonlinear Regression with Dependent Observations," Econometrica, 52, 143-162.

THE GEOMETRY OF MODEL SELECTION IN REGRESSION

Albert Verbeek
Central Bureau of Statistics
Department for Statistical Methods
P.O. Box 959, 2270 AZ Voorburg
The Netherlands

and

University of Utrecht
Sociological Institute
Heidelberglaan 2, 3584 CS Utrecht
The Netherlands

ABSTRACT

This paper deals with the selection of the linear model, i.e. the design matrix X, in linear regression model $Ey=X\beta$. Special cases of this model selection problem are: the selection of predictor variables, selection of transformations, and selection of interactions to be included in the model. The combined process of model selection and parameter estimation is sketched in the classical Neyman-Pearson-Wald framework of mathematical statistics.

1. INTRODUCTION

The topic of this paper is the process of selecting a linear regression model. This model selection process is frequently performed in an iterative, non-formalized way, repeatedly using F tests to arrive eventually at a null hypothesis that is accepted. Both the repeated application of statistical tests and the final acceptance of a null hypothesis violate the basic assumptions underlying statistical test theory. Yet one can reformulate the combined selection and estimation problem in such a way that it largely fits into the classical Neyman-Pearson-Wald framework of the mathematical statistics. The purpose of this paper is precisely to do this. The advantage is, that classical mathematical statistics makes it possible to produce quantitative statements about performances of procedures, at the price of stochastic assumptions and formalization of the procedures.

This paper does not discuss the plethora of algorithms for linear regression model selection; for such a survey see Hocking (1976). Rather it is attempted to describe what these algorithms have in common at a more basic level. To a certain extent an informal data-analytic model search is covered as well. Also note that not the entire model specification problem is treated, only the selection of the linear model, but not the independence of the observations, their variances or other distributional aspects. The following example may clarify this.

Consider the following, four, linear regression model spaces:

M_1: $Ey_i = \beta_1 x_{1i} + \beta_2 x_{2i}$ (i=1,...,n)

M_2: $Ey_i = \beta_1 x_{1i}$ (i=1,...,n)

M_3: $Ey_i = \beta_2 x_{2i}$ (i=1,...,n)

M_4: $Ey_i = 0$ (i=1,...,n) . (1.1)

The term <u>model space</u> is used for M_1 in order to distinguish it from a <u>specific model</u> like

$$Ey_i = -1.39x_{1i} + 0.73x_{2i} \quad (i=1,...,n).$$

In this terminology a model space is a parametrized set of specific models. Note that in this example M_2, M_3, and M_4 are subsets, in fact linear subspaces of M_1 which is a linear subspace of $\mathbf{R}^n$. The dimensions of M_1-M_4 are 2, 1, 1, and 0 respectively. See figure 1, which also shows the estimate $\hat{E}y$ of Ey in model M_1. In fact we will not make any distributional assumptions, but we will just assume that given the linear model, we will have a preferred estimation method e.g. OLS, GLS, or ML. Now every reasonable formal or informal model selection rule will accept M_2 if $\hat{E}y$ is very close to M_2, like in figure 1. So M_2 has a neighbourhood U_2 in $\mathbf{R}^n$ such that no point in U_2-M_2 will be accepted as a final estimate of Ey. The exact size and shape of U_2 of course depends on the particular rule. Similarly we have neighbourhoods U_3 for M_3 and U_4 for M_4, but

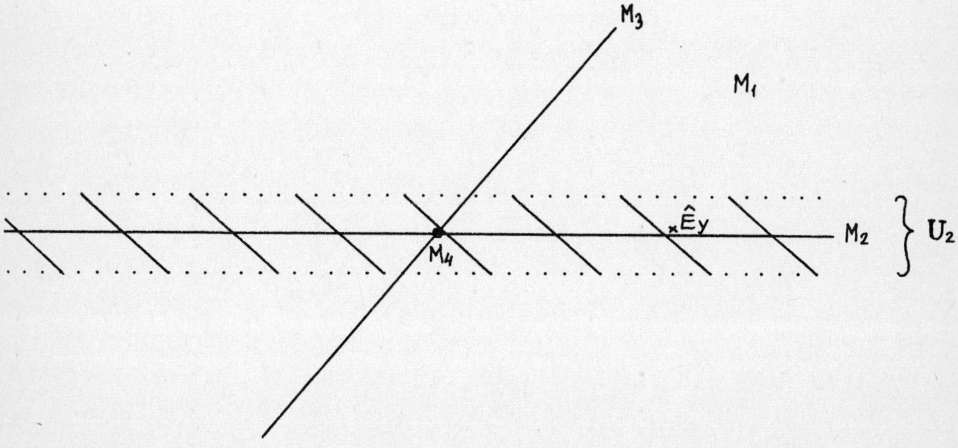

Figure 1. M_2, M_3, M_4 embedded in M_1. The $\hat{E}y$ is the estimate of Ey in M_1

not a neighbourhood U_1 for M_1, because points outside M_1 will not occur as estimates any way. So, put $V_i=U_i-M_i$ (i=2,3,4), and

$$M^* = M_1 - (V_2 \cup V_3 \cup V_4) , \tag{1.2}$$

then M^* (see figure 2) is the set of possible final estimates. Note that each M_i is a linear model in the sense that it is a linear space of possible specific models. But M^* is not a linear space at all, it is not even convex, not even connected. This alone is a sufficient reason to make the model selection problem a difficult one; but it is not the only reason. The entire model selection problem consists of (1) specifying the set $\mathbf{M}$ of possible models, here $\{M_1,\ldots,M_4\}$, (2) the neighbourhoods U_i for each $M_i\in\mathbf{M}$, which determine the set of possible final estimates M^* as in (1.2), and last but not least (3) a set of rules how to deal with intermediate estimates, lying in $\cup V_i$. The discussion of these three choices will be continued in a more general setting in section 2 after the introduction of the necessary definitions and notation.

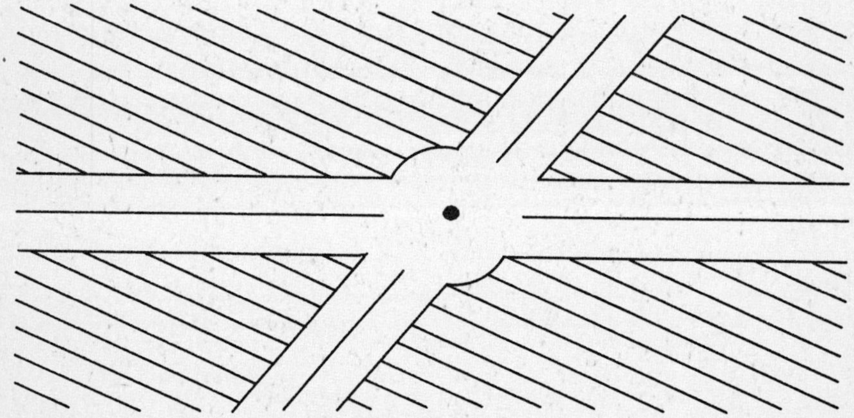

Figure 2. The set M^* as specified by (1.2), consisting of 9 components: 4 shaded areas forming $M_1-(U_2\cup U_3\cup U_4)$, 4 rays forming M_2-U_4 and M_3-U_4, and the point M_4

A useful aid in model selection is the 'deviance-df plot', discussed in section 4. It only requires that $\mathbf{M}$ is specified, and that for each $M_i\in\mathbf{M}$ one has an estimator $\hat{E}y$ of Ey given M_i, and a discrepancy or deviance of the observations y from the estimate $\hat{E}y$. The scatter plot of deviances against degrees of freedom, with one dot for each model, is called dv-df-plot, cf. Figure 3. Some qualitative stochastic properties of this plot are discussed in section 4.

The final section 5 discusses generalizations, e.g. to Nelder-Welderburn-generalized linear models and beyond, and summarizes the conclusions.

2. DEFINITIONS AND NOTATION

The models discussed in this paper are linear regression models

$$Ey_i = \Sigma_j x_{ij}\beta_j \qquad (i=1,\dots,n) , \tag{2.1}$$

with random values y_i, chosen or observed values x_{ij} and unknown β_j $(j=1,\dots,k)$. In vector notation

$$Ey = X\beta , \tag{2.2}$$

We will bypass distributional assumptions by restricting our attention to <u>minimum distance estimation</u> (which of course includes OLS-, GLS- and ML-estimation as special cases.) This is, under regularity conditions, equivalent e.g. to Fisher's equation estimation (Fisher, 1925) and to Huber's M-estimation (Huber, 1981). Moreover, it can also be seen as a data reduction or smoothing technique, rather than as an estimation method. Then $\hat{E}y$ is interpreted as the smoothed value of y, rather than as estimated expected value (cf. subsection 3.2).

The known n×k-matrix X formed by the x_{ij} is called the <u>model matrix</u>. The more popular name 'design matrix' is avoided because it unduely restricts attention to designed experiments, excluding observed or measured X. The j-th column of X will be denoted by x_{*j}. We call the columns X-variables or predictors. Similarly the i-th row vector is x_{i*}. <u>The specification problem under discussion is the choice of the</u> x_{ij}. Important steps in the construction of X are frequently:

- The choice of variables x_{*j} from all variables available. This is widely discussed under the name optimal subset selection, or various other names.
- One-dimensional transformations $\psi(x_{ij})$, $(i=1,\dots,n)$, like log x_{ij}, x_{ij}^2, etc.
- The addition of interactions of available variables. In general these might be defined as transformations $\psi(x_{ij_1},\dots,x_{ij_p})$, $(i=1,\dots,n)$, of more than one variable; here of variables $j_1,\dots j_p$. This is particularly important for categorical X-variables (transformed to dummies) as e.g. in analysis of (co)variance.

Formally the problem may be described as follows. Observation i gives us $z_{i*}=(z_{i1},\dots,z_{i\ell})$ for modelling Ey_i. The specification problem under discussion is the choice of an integer k and of a transformation $\psi:\mathbf{R}^\ell\to\mathbf{R}^k$, such that $x_{i*}=\psi(z_{i*})$ plays the role described in (2.1). The model matrix X corresponding to ψ will be denote by X_ψ. Different ψ correspond to different models possibly with different dimensions k. Note that k may be smaller than ℓ (e.g. for pure subset selection), equal to ℓ (e.g. only one-dimensional transformations), or larger than ℓ (e.g. if interaction terms are added).

Next we define the spaces that allow the 'geometric view' mentioned in the title. Firstly $\mathbf{R}^n$ is the set of all possible realizations of the vector y. Let Ψ be the set of all transformations ψ under consideration. We assume that Ψ is finite. Each $\psi:\mathbf{R}^\ell \to \mathbf{R}^k$ corresponds to a linear subspace (i.e. a model space)

$$M_\psi = \{\Sigma_j x_{*j}\beta_j: x_{i*}=\psi(z_{i*}),\ \beta\in\mathbf{R}^k\} \tag{2.3}$$

of $\mathbf{R}^n$. The set of all M_ψ is denoted by a bold face $\mathbf{M} = \{M_\psi: \psi\in\Psi\}$ and the union is denoted by $M=\cup_{\psi\in\Psi} M_\psi$. We assume that $Ey\in M$. Finally, let L be the linear space generated by M. Let $\mathbf{X}$ be the matrix obtained by joining all X_ψ, $\psi\in\Psi$. The order of the columns in $\mathbf{X}$ is not particularly important, but we do not duplicate identical columns from different X_ψ. The number of columns of $\mathbf{X}$ is called K. It is assumed that no X_ψ has collinearities, but this does not exclude the possibility that $\mathbf{X}$ is collinear or nearly collinear. Note that the column space of $\mathbf{X}$ is L.

Example

Consider optimal subset selection in regression analysis without constant term, where we want to choose only one of the K available predictor variables. Here each M_ψ is a one-dimensional linear subspace of $\mathbf{R}^n$, M is the union of these K rays, and L is the K-dimensional spaces spanned by these rays.

We will assume the following convenient regularity condition on $\mathbf{M}=\{M_\psi:\psi\in\Psi\}$:

$$M_1 \in \mathbf{M} \quad \text{and} \quad M_2 \in \mathbf{M} \quad \text{implies} \quad M_1 \cap M_2 \in \mathbf{M}\,. \tag{2.4}$$

This condition warrants that for any $Ey\in M$, there is a unique, smallest $M_1\in\mathbf{M}$ containing Ey.

For a model space M_ψ the number of degrees of freedom is $df(M_\psi) = n - \dim M_\psi$. A model space M_ψ with $M_\psi=\mathbf{R}^n$ is called saturated. The linear subspace generated by the vector of ones is called the grand mean model space or constant model space. Often these are the two extremal model spaces under consideration.

Furthermore we assume that we are given a distance function dv on $\mathbf{R}^n$, called discrepancy or deviance (cf. Baker and Nelder, 1978, and Aicken, 1983), with the following three properties:

$$dv: \mathbf{R}^n \times \mathbf{R}^n \to [0,\infty] \tag{2.5}$$

$$dv(y,y) = 0 \tag{2.6}$$

for each linear subspace $M \subset \mathbf{R}^n$ and for each point $y \in \mathbf{R}^n$ there is a unique $v \in M$ minimizing $\{dv(y,w): w \in M\}$. (2.7)

Often additional differentiability conditions are imposed on dv, especially for studying asymptotic properties of this function $y \to v$. This function, which maps $\mathbf{R}^n$ onto M_ψ, will be denoted by $P_\psi(y)=v$. It is called the 'minimum-dv estimator'. Famous deviances are (squared) Euclidean distance, yielding OLS, and $dv=G^2=-2$ log likelihood ratio of M to the saturated model S_{obs}, yielding ML-estimation. We do not require dv to be metric; in particular dv need not be symmetric and need not satisfy the triangle inequality. It easily follows from (2.5)-(2.7) that $P_\psi^2=P_\psi$, i.e. P_ψ is a projection (not necessarily linear though!).

Finally each model space M_ψ has a neighbourhood U_ψ in $\mathbf{R}^n$ such that any intermediate estimate $\hat{E}y \in U_\psi - M_\psi$ will be rejected in favour of an estimate in M_ψ. As in the introduction we put $V_\psi = U_\psi - M_\psi$ and $M^* = (M - \cup_{\psi \in \Psi} V_\psi)$. So M^* is the set of acceptable (final) estimates $\hat{E}y$. But note that the combined model selection and estimation process is not simply minimum dv-estimation with respect to M^*! Look again at figure 2. A point in U_2 very close to $M_1 - U_2$ is nevertheless drawn to M_2 rather than to M_1, by definition of U_2. Also note that the neigbourhoods U_ψ will in general not be open. Each point $z \in \mathbf{R}^n$ belongs to a minimal $M_{\psi'}$ (if assumption 2.4 holds). And in general inclusion of z in U_ψ depends on $dv(z,M_\psi)$ which usually is a continuous function, and on $df(M_{\psi'})$ which is a discontinuous function.

3. STOCHASTICS, DATA ANALYSIS OR BOTH

3.1. Stochastics

Section 2 presented the classical, mathematical statistical point of view: y is a stochastic n-vector and

$$Ey = X_\psi \beta \in M_\psi \subset M \, . \tag{3.1}$$

I.e. the parameter to be estimated is Ey, or equivalently the pair

$$(\psi,\beta) \tag{3.2}$$

where β corresponds to $x_{i*}=\psi(z_{i*})$; different ψ's go together with entirely different β's. Stated differently, the set of possible (ψ,β) is not a cartesian product.

If the matrix $\mathbf{X}$ of all possible predictors has no (near) collinearities, each $Ey\in M$ can be expressed in a unique way as

$$Ey = \mathbf{X}\boldsymbol{\beta} = X_{\psi}\beta \ , \tag{3.3}$$

where $\boldsymbol{\beta}$ is obtained by padding β with zeroes. So the distribution of a reasonable estimator $\hat{\boldsymbol{\beta}}$ will be of a mixed type: partly continuous, partly discrete. Most components of $\hat{\boldsymbol{\beta}}$ will have a positive probability of being zero. This means that VAR $\hat{\boldsymbol{\beta}}$ alone does not give a very complete picture of the variation. Also $\hat{\boldsymbol{\beta}}$ will in general not be nearly multinormally distributed. If $\mathbf{X}$ is nearly collinear while each X_{ψ} is not, no simple representation like (3.3) is possible, and consequently it seems impossible to define something like VAR $\hat{\beta}$ or confidence intervals for β.

In practice, one usually chooses a number of candidate models ψ (called intermediate estimates in this paper), obtains the corresponding $\hat{Ey}$ or $\hat{\beta}$ and judges the fit. This proces may reiterate. Then somehow one chooses the (final) estimate $\hat{\psi}$ and the corresponding $\hat{Ey}$ and $\hat{\beta}$. For each model most reporting of standard errors, tests and confidence intervals ignores the estimation of ψ. This tradition is so widely accepted that there exist no generally accepted measures for the quality of an estimator $(\hat{\psi},\hat{\beta})$. Yet these are fairly easily defined. Important measures for the quality of $(\hat{\psi},\hat{\beta})$ are given in (3.4)-(3.8), where $Ey=X_{\psi_0}\beta_0$ denotes the true specific model, and M_{ψ_0} the smallest model space containing Ey (cf. (2.4):

$$\Pr(\hat{\psi}=\psi_0) \ , \tag{3.4}$$

$$\Pr(M_{\psi_0}\subset M_{\hat{\psi}}) = \Pr(Ey\in M_{\hat{\psi}}) \tag{3.5}$$

$$\mathrm{VAR}(\hat{\beta}\,|\,\hat{\psi}=\psi_0) \ , \tag{3.6}$$

or more globally by

$$E(dv(\hat{Ey},M_{\psi_0})) \ , \tag{3.7}$$

$$E(dv(\hat{Ey},Ey)) \ , \tag{3.8}$$

The difference between (3.4) and (3.5) is that (3.5) allows the presence of predictors in the estimated model space that are not necessary. Consequently (3.5) is larger than (3.4).

A formula like (3.8) comes close to the criteria used in prediction analysis. Here the goal of model selection is the construction of a predictor for the next y, for which x (or z) is already given, and which is (conditionally on x or z) independent of the training sample obtained so far. See e.g. Seber (1977, section 12.2.(d)). It is also worthwhile to note that optimization of (3.8) may conflict with optimization of (3.4). E.g., in prediction analysis a model simpler than the true model may yield better, more stable and more robust estimates of Ey (cf. Dijkstra, 1983, and Steerneman, 1983).

Under GLS-estimation and the assumption L=M we may approximate $p_\psi = Pr(\hat{\psi}=\psi)$ by

$$p_\psi \doteq Pr(\hat{Ey} \in U_\psi) , \tag{3.9}$$

where $\hat{Ey}$ is the GLS-estimate corresponding to L=M, and U_ψ is as defined at the end of section 2. Under the additional assumptions that each U_ψ is determined by linear or quadratic constraints and that y has a multinormal distribution that is accurately known, the right-hand side of (3.9) is fairly easy to obtain. This may be useful, (1) in simulation studies, (2) in the analysis of so large a sample that $\hat{Ey}$ (the estimate in L) is accurately known, and (3) in the planning stage when number of observations and power are studied for a number of hypothetical specific models.

If the estimation of ψ is completely formalized (= well defined, like 'stepwise regression with such-and-such parameters') and if the sample size is large, then (3.4)-(3.8) are easily estimated by bootstrapping. I.e. one first estimates the population distribution via a model with very many parameters, like L, and then simulates the model selection and estimation process as if this estimate is the population distribution. Under the assumption that (3.4)-(3.8) have not too much variation as functions of the population distribution, this gives good estimates for the true values of (3.4)-(3.8). For more details, see e.g. Efron (1982).

More stochastic properties of $\hat{\psi}$, $\hat{\beta}$ and $\hat{Ey}$ will be discussed in subsection 3.3 and in section 4.

3.2. Data analysis

A somewhat different point of view, briefly indicated in section 2 is taken in data analysis. Here $y_1,\ldots,y_n$ are interpreted as non-stochastic, population data, and $X\beta$ is seen as a specific smoothed model for y. Also in this case there is an 'a priori' space of possible outcomes $\mathbf{R}^n$ and sets M_ψ, $\psi\in\Psi$, of possible smoothed models. The definitions and the framework from section 2 completely carry over to this case, with two related exceptions:

- there is no expectation operator E; rather $\hat{E}$ is interpreted as smoothing operator;
- the residuals $y-\hat{E}y$ are not modelled by a stochastic model; they are not modelled at all!

In this view data analysis, smoothing, filtering and data reduction are roughly synonymous. They are more general than the models from mathematical statistics, in the sense that they require less assumptions. And they are correspondingly less powerful. It is only assumed and hoped for that $\hat{E}y$ robustly captures 'the salient structure of the data', while any structure in the residuals is of a much smaller magnitude. Hence the information in the residuals can be summarized by a single measure of dispersion. C.f. Tukey's emphasis on the decomposition data=fit+residual, e.g. in Tukey (1977).

Just as in subsection 3.1 one has different model spaces M_ψ. More parsimonious models are easier to interpret, and tend to be more robust, in Tukey's sense of resistence against small changes in all data and large changes in a few data. But in general they provide less accurate approximations; i.e. $dv(y,\hat{E}y)$ is larger. In the stochastic framework maximization of the quality of $(\hat{\psi},\hat{\beta})$ in terms of (3.4)-(3.8), may provide a basis; in data analysis we need subject matter information to provide a yardstick to compare differences in parsimony (say: in degrees of freedom) to differences in deviances.

3.3. A unified approach

In many applications it is possible and useful to reconcile the stochastic and data analytic views presented in subsections 3.1 and 3.2: Interpret y as a stochastic n-vector for which (3.1) only holds approximately. As in 3.2 we may wish to trade some accuracy and unbiasedness for a gain in simplicity, and as in 3.2 we need help from the interpretation for making this trade off. The rules derived from hypothesis testing however do not use subject matter information.

The model selection and estimation problem now can be formulated as follows:

(i) Choose $\mathbf{M}=\{M_\psi:\psi\in\Psi\}$, guided by subject matter information.

(ii) Choose $\{U_\psi:\psi\in\Psi\}$, guided both by subject matter information and by the size of sampling errors. Next V_ψ, and M^* are defined as in section 2.

(iii) Define an estimator $\mathbf{R}^n \to M^*$.

In my view the model selection problem is difficult for two reasons. Step (i) is the least difficult. The difficulty of step (ii) lies in the formalization of the desired degree of accuracy. This step is much neglected. And the difficulty of step (iii) is of mathematical nature; as pointed out in the introduction $Ey\in M_{\psi_0}$ is a linear model, and hence well understood, but $Ey\in M^*$ is very much non-linear. Even from a purely technical, mathematical point of view the construction of a good estimator, its computation and the derivation of its properties pose many difficult problems.

4. DEVIANCE-DEGREE-OF-FREEDOM PLOTS

4.1. Definition

This section presents rather informal and qualitative discussions of the estimation of ψ. Given the observations y important properties of a model space M_ψ are its deviance $dv(y,M_\psi)$ and its parsimony. In this section we measure parsimony through the number of degrees of freedom, df, but one may substitute any other one-dimensional measure at will. Of course, residuals and other properties of $\hat{E}y$ are important too, but dv and df already contain very important information. This is conveniently represented in a dv-df scatterplot, where each M_ψ is represented as the point $(dv(y,M_\psi), df(M_\psi))$, see figure 3. Good models have small dv and many df, i.e. they are in the south eastern part of the plot. Models on the south eastern boundary of the convex hull, might be called 'admissible'.

4.2. Trade-off between deviance and degrees of freedom

In order to choose a model space from the admissible set, we have to specify 'how much deviance we are prepared to pay for a certain gain in df'. In other words, we need the dv-df-indifference lines. Two popular rules for preferring $model_1$ over $model_2$ with $df_1>df_2$ are:

$$dv_1 - dv_2 < \chi^2_{df_1-df_2}(0.95) \tag{4.1}$$

and

$$(dv_1-dv_2)/(df_1-df_2) < c \, . \tag{4.2}$$

Mallows (1973), Sakamoto and Akaike (1978) and Dijkstra (1984) propagate c=2, which is also the default in BMDP9R (Dixon and Frane, 1977), one of the superior regression subset selection programs. If the indifference lines are defined by (4.2), this defines a line segment or a point of the admissible set; see figure 3.

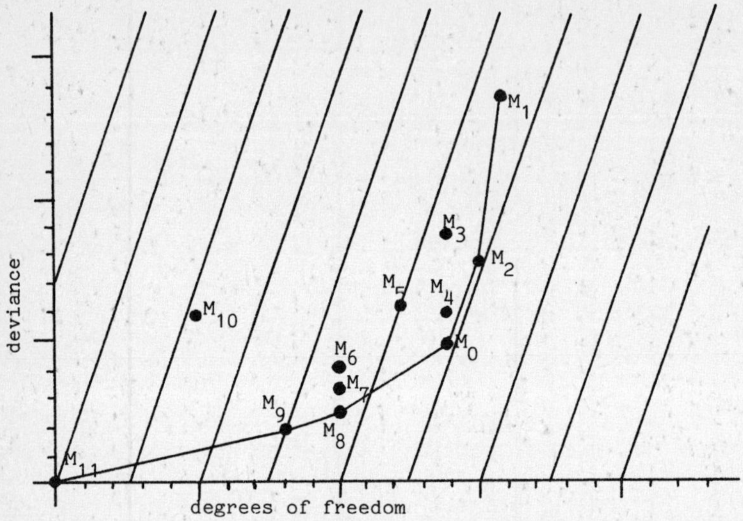

Figure 3. A dv-df-plot for 11 models. The admissable models are on the drawn polygon which is the south-east boundary of the convex hull; the dv-df-indifference lines are given by (4.2) with c=3. The optimal models are M_0 and M_2

4.3. Stochastic properties of the dv-df-plot

In this subsection we take the point of view of subsections 3.1 or 3.3; y is a stochastic vector and the dv-df-plot of k models can be represented as a stochastic 2k-vector. First we distinguish three types of models:

(i) The smallest model $M_{\psi_0} \in \mathbf{M}$ with $Ey \in M_{\psi_0}$. This is called the true model. Its existence is guaranteed by assumption (2.4). We write $\nu_0 = df(M_{\psi_0})$.

(ii) The models M_ψ containing M_{ψ_0}, and a fortiori Ey. These are called overcomplete. Their df are less than ν_0.

(iii) The 'incorrect' models, not containing Ey. If $df(M_\psi) > \nu_0$ then M_ψ is necessarily incorrect. But if M_ψ is incorrect, its df may also be equal to or larger than ν_0.

Consider figure 3. Knowing that M_0 is the true model, M_1-M_4 and possibly M_{10} are incorrect. The saturated model M_{11} is trivially overcomplete, and probably also M_6-M_9 are. But we can only be sure if we know the true model. For an incorrect model M_ψ we define the non-centrality as

$$\lambda_\psi = dv(Ey, M_\psi) \; . \tag{4.3}$$

For the true and the overcomplete models the non-centrality is zero. Next we make four simplifying assumptions (4.4)-(4.7). The first three assumptions hold exactly or approximately in many applications.

The distribution of y, conditional on x, is multinormal , (4.4)

if $Ey \in M_\psi$, then $dv(y,M_\psi)$ is χ^2_ν-distributed with $\nu = df(M_\psi)$, (4.5)

if $Ey \notin M_\psi$, then $E\, dv(y,M_\psi) = df(M_\psi) + \lambda_\psi$. (4.6)

The final assumption is the most stringent.

For all $M_\psi \in \mathbf{M}$ either $\lambda_\psi = 0$ or $\lambda_\psi > 4\sqrt{df(M_\psi)}$ (4.7)

It essentially means that the estimation of ψ_0 is fairly straightforward; each model either fits (in the sense that $Ey \in M_\psi$) or it fits so poorly, that we have a fair chance of detecting this, even if simultaneous testing methods are used. The factor 4 in (4.6) is only a crude figure; note that by (4.5) the standard deviation of $dv(y,M_\psi)$ is $\sqrt{(2 * df(M_\psi))}$, if M_ψ fits.

Next we partition $\mathbf{M}$ according to df. Define

$$\mathbf{M}_\nu = \{M \in \mathbf{M} : df(M) = \nu\} \; . \tag{4.8}$$

We will separately discuss $\mathbf{M}_\nu$'s containing overcomplete models, $\mathbf{M}_{\nu_0}$, and $\mathbf{M}_\nu$'s only containing incorrect models.

Suppose $\mathbf{M}_\nu$ contains k overcomplete models M_ψ. For each of these

$$dv((y,M_\psi) \sim \chi^2_\nu \tag{4.9}$$

by (4.6). If $\mathbf{M}_\nu$ produces an admissible model (see figure 3), then it must have the smallest deviance in $\mathbf{M}_\nu$. By (4.7) any incorrect model stands a small chance to be $\mathbf{M}_\nu$-champion. So we ignore these. Then the minimal deviance in $\mathbf{M}_\nu$ is distributed as the minimum of k χ^2_ν-variates. If these are independent, we can approximate this minimal deviance as follows:

$$E \min\{dv(y,M): M \in \mathbf{M}_\nu\} \doteq \text{the } 1/(k+1)\text{-quantile of } \chi^2_\nu \; . \qquad (4.10)$$

If they are positively correlated, as often happens, the expected minimal deviance is closer to ν, but if $k>1$ it is always smaller than ν:

$$E \min\{dv(y,M): M \in \mathbf{M}_\nu\} < \nu \; . \qquad (4.11)$$

Next consider $\mathbf{M}_{\nu_0}$. It contains the true model; so any other model in $\mathbf{M}_{\nu_0}$ must be incorrect, because no model can contain the true model and have the same number of df. Again by (4.7) we may assume that with high probability

$$\min\{dv(\phi(y),M): M \in \mathbf{M}_{\nu_0}\} = dv(\phi(y),M_{\psi_0}) \sim \chi^2_{\nu_0} \; . \qquad (4.12)$$

So approximately

$$E \min\{dv(\phi(y),M): M \in \mathbf{M}_{\nu_0}\} = \nu_0 \; . \qquad (4.13)$$

Finally we consider the remaining $\mathbf{M}_\nu$ containing only incorrect models. In general their non-centralities will be pairwise different, and there will be much less competition for these $\mathbf{M}_\nu$-minimal deviances than in $\mathbf{M}_\nu$'s containing overcomplete models. Only the models with a non-centrality close to the one with the smallest non-centrality will compete. If the smallest non-centrality is much smaller than the next smallest, then

$$E \min\{dv(\phi(y),M): M \in \mathbf{M}_\nu\} = \nu + \min\{\lambda_\psi : M_\psi \in \mathbf{M}_\nu\} \; ; \qquad (4.14)$$

otherwise, the left hand side will be smaller than the right hand side.

If (4.10), (4.13) and (4.14) are good approximations, this provides important information on the slope of the south eastern boundary of the convex hull of the models in the dv-df-plot, cf. figure 3. Of course, this boundary itself is a concave function of df; so the slope is a non-decreasing function of df. At ν_0 the expected slope is larger than 1; this holds for the left hand derivative and for the right hand derivative as well. How much larger than 1 depends grossly on two factors:

- the number of overcomplete models with df slightly below ν_0;
- the non-centrality of models with df slightly above ν_0.

If the model selection and estimation problem is specified as in subsection 3.3, (i)-(iii), and if (4.4)-(4.7) are satisfied, then it is not too difficult to obtain numerical results on the distribution of the dv-df-plot for a hypothesized value of Ey, or for a bootstrap estimate. This falls short of solving the inferential problem, but it does give new insights.

4.4. The directed graph of alternative models

Several heuristic algorithms for model selection depend only on the deviances and degrees of freedom of the models under consideration, and on the inclusion relation between model spaces. (Note that hitherto the latter relation was ignored in our discussion of the dv-df-plot!) For such algorithms the following representation can be useful. Consider the directed graph of which the vertices are the model spaces plotted in the dv-df-plot. (Each model space M_ψ corresponds to one vertex = one point in the plot.) An arc is drawn from $M_1 \in \mathbf{M}$ to $M_2 \in \mathbf{M}$ if and only if $M_2 \subset M_1$. So all arcs have directions in the south west quadrant. If we adopt a rule like (4.2), then next to each arc we may write its weight

$$w = (dv(M_2) - dv(M_1))/(df(M_2) - df(M_1)) \ . \tag{4.15}$$

The weight then measures the extent by which we prefer the smaller model M_2.

Stepwise regression algorithms try to search up or down pathes of this graph along the admissible set. The problem is that model spaces in the admissible set need not be on a path that is everywhere close to the admissible set. Also arcs with a large weight may be on an otherwise uninteresting path. In many practical cases such algorithms provide a quick, and reasonable estimate of the true model. But typically they provide little indication how good a particular solution is. And it is easy to construct examples where they fail completely.

Yet it should also be mentioned that there exist fast algorithms for guaranteedly finding the model on the admissible set with larged dv-c.df (for a given c), without evaluating all (dv,df)'s of all models. Such an algorithm makes the BMDP optimal subset selection program BMDP9R approximately as fast as the BMDP stepwise regression program! (Cf. Dixon and Brown, 1977.)

4.5. Testing goodness-of-fit

A common procedure in model selection is the F test. Two fundamental principles of the classical Neyman-Pearson test theory are violated in this usage. The first violation is the repeated usage of these tests on many models, as if they were single, isolated tests. The second violation is the search for an H_0 that is not rejected; one looks for a model that fits, and eventually chooses such a model. In a sense one 'proves' this model to be acceptable. But test theory does not allow the conclusion that H_0 is true; at best it allows only the conclusion that H_0 does not conflict with current data. These violations deprive this usage of test theory of its formal justification. Whether or not such usage leads to poor decision rules remains an open question.

In principle it is sometimes possible to solve the first problem mentioned above by the application of simultaneous testing theory (see e.g. Miller, 1981). Suppose there exists a largest model space amongst all competitive model spaces (i.e. M=L). Then one may find an $(1-\alpha)$-confidence region for Ey in this model, and require the final estimates to lie in this region. All models in this region are said to fit well, and no further testing is performed. Within this region one optimizes a balance between deviance and parsimony.

There are two more sturdy methods available for the assessment of the quality of the model selection and estimation procedure. The first one is bootstrapping, as briefly discussed in subsection 3.1. This is applicable only if the model selection procedure is completely formalized, i.e. if it is easily repeated for freshly generated, simulated data. The second method is crossvalidation. Crossvalidation is a very powerful and somewhat neglected tool, that also applies to model selection processes that are not formalized. Before the analysis commences one splits the data in two parts, called 'pool' and 'mirror'. The mirror data are set aside until a model estimate $\hat{\Psi}$ and a parameter estimate $\hat{\beta}$ have been fished out of the pool data. Then the deviance is estimated by confronting the estimated model $(\hat{\Psi},\hat{\beta})$ with the mirror data. If all data are independent observations, one has as many degrees of freedom as the size of the mirror data. Personally I often work with mirror sizes in the range 50-200 observations for samples of total size 200-2000. The sample size of the mirror data is directly related to the accuracy of the deviance estimated from these. The sample size of the pool should be large enough to give sufficient protection against overfitting. Needless to say that the choice of the relative sizes of pool and mirror is rather subjective. The selection of the mirror data also merits careful thought. A simple strategy is to take a simple random sample. But if one chooses non-randomly, by selecting on a variable not included in the model (like: interviewer), one can also incorporate some of the systematic errors into the deviance estimated from the miror data. Finally we should mention one difficulty with cross-validation. If the cross-validation estimate of the deviance shows a very poor fit, then we are left empty handed. Of course one cannot reiterate and analyse the data once again without a serious danger of overfitting.

5. DISCUSSION

In this paper we sketched the combined process of model selection (i.e. model estimation) and parameter estimation for linear regression models. This has lead to the following conclusions.

- The set M^* of possible (final) estimates $\hat{Ey}$ is not linear and not connected. Although each regression model under discussion is linear, the regression model selection problem is highly non-linear.
- The definition of M^* also depends on arguments balancing the profits of simplicity against the profits of goodness of fit or precision. This balancing should not automatically be done only by hypothesis testing, because two fundamental assumptions are violated.
- Given M^* the estimation problem is still non-trivial; minimum-dv estimation with respect to M^* is not consistent with the definitions of V_ψ and M^*.
- Var $\hat{\beta}$ is not defined or not very useful for assessing the quality of $\hat{\beta}$. Rather (3.4)-(3.8) should be used. Useful estimates can be obtained either by bootstrapping or by cross-validation.
- Simple approximations provide helpful insights in the stochastic behaviour of dv-df-plots, cf. (4.10)-(4.14).

A lot of work remains to be done. The definition of the U_ψ should be worked out for various particular formal model selection procedures. Properties of the quality measures (3.4)-(3.8) should be investigated. The quality of the approximations applied in subsection 4.3 should be worked out, etc.

Also, generalizations are possible. It is easy to generalize the present discussion to Nelder-Wedderburn's generalized linear models, see Nelder and Wedderburn (1972) or Aicken (1983). But still further generalizations are possible. Crucial to the present discussion is the concept of minimum deviance estimation. If Y is the space of possible observations y, and M is the space of possible parameter values μ, then one should have a deviance $dv(y,\mu)$ defined on $Y \times M$, satisfying (2.5)-(2.7). Models can be arbitrary or special subset of M, such as linear subspaces.

An important question that has hardly been discussed is the choice of the U_ψ. We have critizied the automatic determination of U_ψ by goodness-of-fit tests in 4.5. But we have not offered an alternative. Sometimes the subject matter helps to assess which differences are too small to be of practical interest; and this may lead to useful U_ψ. A rule of thumb along these lines is being worked out in Verbeek (in preparation).

ACKNOWLEDGEMENTS

The author greatfully acknowledges valuable comments and suggestions from many colleagues, particularly from Dijkstra, Weesie, Molenaar, Koster, Wansbeek, and Boomsma. The drawings have been made by Imre Kortbeek.

REFERENCES

Aicken, M., 1983, Linear statistical analysis of discrete data (Wiley, New York).
Baker, R.J. and J.A. Nelder, 1978, The GLIM system, release 3 (Numerical Algorithm Group, Oxford).
Dijkstra, T.K., 1983, Misspecification and the choice of estimators, a heuristic approach (This volume).
Dixon, W.J. and M.B. Brown, eds., 1977, BMDP-77, Biomedical computer programs P-series (University of California Press, Los Angeles).
Efron, B., 1982, The jacknife, the bootstrap and other resampling plans (Society for Industrial and Applied Mathematics, Philadelphia).
Fisher, R.A., 1925, Theory of statistical estimation. Procedings of the Cambridge Philosophical Society 22, pp. 700-725.
Hocking, R.R., 1976, The analysis and selection of variables in linear regression, Biometrics 32, pp. 1-50.
Huber, J.P., 1981, Robust statistics (Wiley, New York).
Mallows, C.L., 1973, Some comments on C_p, Technometrics 15, pp. 661-675.
Miller, R.G., 1981, Simultaneous statistical inference, second edition (Springer Verlag, Heidelberg).
Nelder, J.A. and R.W.M. Wedderburn, 1972, Generalized linear models. Journal of the Royal Statistical Society A 153, pp. 370-384.
Sakamoto, Y. and H. Akaike, 1978, Analysis of cross-classified data by AIC. Annals of the Institute of Mathematical Statistics 30, pp. 185-198.
Seber, G.A.F., 1977, Linear regression analysis (Wiley, New York).
Steerneman, A.G.M. 1983, Prediction performance and the number of variables in multivariate linear regression (this volume).
Tukey, J.W., 1977, Exploratory data analysis (Addison-Wesley, New York).
Verbeek, A., in preparation, Goodness-of-fit testing or estimating the deviance in log-linear modelling? Internal CBS-report (Netherlands Central Bureau of Statistics, Voorburg).

MISSPECIFICATION AND THE CHOICE OF ESTIMATORS, A HEURISTIC APPROACH

Theo K. Dijkstra
Econometrics Institute
University of Groningen
P.O. Box 800, 9700 AV Groningen
The Netherlands

0. ABSTRACT

We study a classical simultaneous system which is possibly misspecified in the sense that too many variables may have been deleted from the structural equations. Suppose the system is to be used for predictive purposes. We compare unrestricted least squares, full-information and pre-test estimators based on the outcome of a chi-square test-statistic. A plea is made to take two times the degrees of freedom of the hypothesized model as critical value for the chi-square test.

1. INTRODUCTION

Consider a classical simultaneous system of equations in which a set of endogenous variables is related linearly to a set of exogenous variables plus residuals. If the system is to be used for predictive purposes, it seems reasonable to try to estimate the systematic, non-random, part of the endogenous variables with minimum mean squared error. Let us allow for the possibility that the system is misspecified in the sense that the matrices of the structural form may contain too many zeroes. We will show that if the specification error is small it will still be worthwhile to impose the incorrect model upon the data *and* to use full-information estimation methods. However, with large specification errors it is clearly advisable to estimate the systematic part using unrestricted least squares. In many practical situations knowledge about the specification error will not be precise enough to be useful, and so one may naturally feel inclined to test the model prior to estimation with some chi-square test: If the fit appears reasonable then use full-information methods, otherwise use unrestricted least squares. The ensuing estimators are called pre-test estimators. As will be seen below, their distributional properties differ markedly from the alternatives mentioned. In fact, whatever the size of the specification error, pre-test estimators are at best second-best. Of crucial importance to their performance however is the critical value of the chi-square test. We will argue that two times the degrees of freedom of the hypothesized model is an (approximately) optimal critical value, in the sense that the maximum difference between the possible performance and what could ideally be had is minimal.

The paper is organized as follows. The next four sections deal mainly with the one-equation linear model as a preparation for the simultaneous system. This part contains the motivations for the adoption of the critical value 'two times the degrees of freedom'. We build on work done by Judge & Bock (1978) and Brook (1976), who analyzed the one-equation linear model with a complete list of explanatory variables and normally distributed residuals. The last two sections extend the analysis to simultaneous systems, section 6 contains the main results and section 7 collects the proofs.

Before proceeding we would like to explain the word 'heuristic' in the title: 1) with respect to the parameters we have not bothered to prove more than pointwise convergence of sampling distributions, 2) we will argue as if properties of limiting, asymptotic, distributions are relevant for finite sample distributions, 3) there are strong indications for the optimality of the suggested critical value but no proof, 4) the choice of loss functions involves an unavoidable element of subjectivity.

Finally, the reader is assumed to be acquainted with the 'vec' notation and matrix differentiation, see e.g. Dhrymes (1978), and with some simple theorems of asymptotic theory, see e.g. Lehmann (1983), Bishop et.al. (1975), Rao (1973) and Malinvaud (1970).

2. THE LINEAR MODEL

Let (X,Z) be a non-stochastic matrix of order $T\times(k+m)$. X is a $T\times k$ matrix with full column rank. The t-th row of (X,Z) will be denoted by (x_t', z_t'), $t = 1,2,\dots,T$. Let y, with typical element y_t, be a $T\times 1$ vector generated by

$$\underline{y}_t = \beta_T' x_t + \gamma_T' z_t + \underline{\varepsilon}_t \tag{1}$$

or

$$\underline{y} = X\beta_T + Z\gamma_T + \underline{\varepsilon}$$

$\beta_T \in \mathbb{R}^k$, $\gamma_T \in \mathbb{R}^m$, the $\underline{\varepsilon}_t$'s are i.i.d. random variables with zero mean and finite variance σ^2 (we will follow the Dutch convention, $\underline{\varepsilon}_t$ distinghuises the random variable from its realization, ε_t). Note that the distribution of $\underline{\varepsilon}$ is not required to belong to a specific parametric family. Consequently, if we want to study stochastic properties of estimators and tests we will have to resort to asymptotic theory. To facilitate this we will adopt the following assumptions:

a) $$\lim_{T\to\infty} \frac{1}{T}\begin{bmatrix} X'X & X'Z \\ & Z'Z \end{bmatrix} = \begin{bmatrix} \Sigma_{xx} & \Sigma_{xz} \\ & \Sigma_{zz} \end{bmatrix} \text{ positive definite} \tag{2}$$

We note for further reference two useful consequences which belong to the standard asymptotic theory for linear models, see e.g. Malinvaud (1970, ch. 6)

$$\frac{1}{\sqrt{T}}X'\underline{\varepsilon} \xrightarrow{L} \mathcal{N}(0,\sigma^2\Sigma_{xx})$$

and (3)

$$\frac{1}{\sqrt{T}}Z'\underline{\varepsilon} \xrightarrow{L} \mathcal{N}(0,\sigma^2\Sigma_{zz})$$

b) $\gamma_T = \frac{1}{\sqrt{T}}\gamma$, $\beta_T = \beta_o + \frac{1}{\sqrt{T}}\delta$ (4)

$R\beta_o = r$

R is a known $q\times k$ matrix of rank q, r is a known $q\times 1$ vector and β_o,δ are some vectors of order $k\times 1$.

The dependence of γ_T and β_T on T has the advantage that the asymptotic power of a test to be described below will be less than one when using a fixed critical value (see Bishop et.al. (1975) ch. 14, Sen (1979), Stroud (1971) or Fix et.al. (1959)). An asymptotic power equal to one would lead to rather trivial results in the context of this paper.

At this point it is convenient to note that

$$\beta_T^* \equiv \beta_T + (X'X)^{-1}X'Z\gamma_T \tag{5}$$

minimizes $E(\underline{y}-X\beta)'(\underline{y}-X\beta)$ for all $\beta \in \mathbb{R}^k$, or equivalently β_T^* solves $\min_{\beta \in \mathbb{R}^k} \|X\beta-(X\beta_T+Z\gamma_T)\|$. So $X\beta_T^*$ is the best (least squares) approximation of the systematic part of $\underline{y}$ in terms of X.

Suppose now that a researcher, unaware of the presence of $Z\gamma_T$ in (1), or unable to obtain Z, decides to estimate the systematic part of $\underline{y}$ by means of a linear combination of the columns of X. This can be done in many ways of course. We will compare a few possibilities using as a measure of quality the average squared distance to $E\underline{y}$, divided by σ^2, or equivalently, the average squared distance to $X\beta_T^*$, divided by σ^2. This is equivalent since the difference between the two quality measures is the same for all estimators considered, as will be easy to verify.

A simple estimator which suggests itself is $X\underline{b}$ where $\underline{b} = (X'X)^{-1}X'\underline{y}$. Since $\underline{b}$ can be written as $\beta_T^* + (X'X)^{-1}X'\underline{\varepsilon}$ we have

$$E(\underline{b}-\beta_T^*) = 0,\ E(\underline{b}-\beta_T^*)(\underline{b}-\beta_T^*)' = \sigma^2(X'X)^{-1}$$

and also, which will be useful later on,

$$\sqrt{T}(\underline{b}-\beta_T^*) \xrightarrow{L} \mathcal{N}(0,\sigma^2\Sigma_{xx}^{-1}) \tag{6}$$

Consequently,

$$\frac{1}{\sigma^2}E(X\underline{b}-X\beta_T^*)'(X\underline{b}-X\beta_T^*) = \frac{1}{\sigma^2}\mathrm{tr}\ X'X.\sigma^2(X'X)^{-1} = k$$

Alternatively, one could minimize $(b-\beta)'X'X(b-\beta)$ subject to $R\beta = r$ for all $\beta \in \mathbb{R}^k$. This yields $\hat{\beta}$, say, which can be written as

$$b - (X'X)^{-1}R'[R(X'X)^{-1}R']^{-1}(Rb-r)$$

So with a little manipulation,

$$\underline{\hat{\beta}}-\beta_T^* = -(X'X)^{-1} R'(R(X'X)^{-1}R')^{-1}. \frac{1}{\sqrt{T}}R(\delta+(X'X)^{-1}X'Z\gamma)$$
$$+ (X'X)^{-1}[X'X-R'(R(X'X)^{-1}R')^{-1}R](X'X)^{-1}X'\underline{\varepsilon} \tag{7}$$

The mean of $\underline{\hat{\beta}}-\beta_T^*$ is of course just the first part of this lenghty expression not involving $\underline{\varepsilon}$. The covariance matrix of $\underline{\hat{\beta}}$ equals

$$\sigma^2[(X'X)^{-1}-(X'X)^{-1}R'(R(X'X)^{-1}R')^{-1}R(X'X)^{-1}] \tag{8}$$

and we have

$$\sqrt{T}(\underline{\hat{\beta}}-\beta_T^*) \xrightarrow{L} \mathcal{N}(-\Sigma_{xx}^{-1}R'(R\Sigma_{xx}^{-1}R')^{-1}R(\delta+\Sigma_{xx}^{-1}\Sigma_{xz}\gamma),$$
$$\sigma^2[\Sigma_{xx}^{-1}-\Sigma_{xx}^{-1}R'(R\Sigma_{xx}^{-1}R')^{-1}R\Sigma_{xx}^{-1}]) \tag{9}$$

Now (7) and (8) imply that

$$\frac{1}{\sigma^2}E(X\underline{\hat{\beta}}-X\beta_T^*)'(X\underline{\hat{\beta}}-X\beta_T^*) = (k-q) + \lambda_T$$

where λ_T,'the size of the specification error', equals by definition

$$\lambda_T = (\delta+(X'X)^{-1}X'Z\gamma)'R'(R(\frac{X'X}{T})^{-1}R')^{-1}R(\delta+(X'X)^{-1}X'Z\gamma)/\sigma^2 \tag{10}$$

We deduce that it pays to simplify by means of the q independent restrictions if and only if $\lambda_T < q$ (see also Judge & Bock (1978)). However, this result is not very helpful since for obvious reasons knowledge about λ_T will not be abundant. But there is a strong and useful relationship between λ_T and the familiar 'F'-test statistic which we will write as $\frac{1}{q}\underline{u}_T$ with

$$\underline{u}_T \equiv \frac{(R\underline{b}-r)'(R(X'X)^{-1}R')^{-1}(R\underline{b}-r)}{\underline{s}^2} \tag{11}$$

or

$$\underline{u}_T \equiv \frac{(\underline{\hat{\beta}}-\underline{b})'X'X(\underline{\hat{\beta}}-\underline{b})}{\underline{s}^2} \tag{12}$$

where

$$\underline{s}^2 \equiv \frac{1}{T-k}(\underline{y}-X\underline{b})'(\underline{y}-X\underline{b}) \tag{13}$$

In fact we have

$$\underline{u}_T \xrightarrow{L} \chi^2(q,\lambda) \tag{14}$$

with

$$\lambda \equiv \lim_{T\to\infty} \lambda_T = (\delta+\Sigma_{xx}^{-1}\Sigma_{xz}\gamma)'R'(R\Sigma_{xx}^{-1}R')^{-1}R(\delta+\Sigma_{xx}^{-1}\Sigma_{xz}\gamma)/\sigma^2 \tag{15}$$

To prove this observe that

$$\sqrt{T}(R\underline{b}-r) = R(\delta+(X'X)^{-1}X'Z\gamma) + R(\frac{X'X}{T})^{-1}\frac{X'\varepsilon}{\sqrt{T}}$$

$$\xrightarrow{L} \mathcal{N}(R(\delta+\Sigma_{xx}^{-1}\Sigma_{xz}\gamma),\sigma^2 R\Sigma_{xx}^{-1}R')$$

Also, with $M \equiv I - X(X'X)^{-1}X'$, $\underline{s}^2 = \frac{1}{T-k}(Z\frac{\gamma}{\sqrt{T}}+\underline{\varepsilon})'M(Z\frac{\gamma}{\sqrt{T}}+\underline{\varepsilon}) = \frac{1}{T-k}[\frac{1}{T}\gamma'Z'MZ\gamma+\underline{\varepsilon}'M\underline{\varepsilon}+$ $+2\gamma'Z'\frac{M\underline{\varepsilon}}{\sqrt{T}}] \xrightarrow{P} 0 + \sigma^2 + 0 = \sigma^2$ because of (2) and (3).

Therefore, $\frac{1}{\underline{s}^2}(R(\frac{X'X}{T})^{-1}R')^{-1}$ tends in probability to the inverse of the asymptotic covariance matrix of $\sqrt{T}(R\underline{b}-r)$, and the result is implied by the definition of the non-central χ^2-distribution and standard asymptotic theorems, see. e.g. Rao (1973).

From (14) it follows that $\underline{u}_T$ is approximately distributed as $\chi^2(q,\lambda_T)$ with $E\underline{u}_T \approx q + \lambda_T$. We can use this fact to estimate λ_T with $u_T - q$ or with $\max(u_T - q,0)$. If $\underline{u}_T \sim \chi^2(q,\lambda_T)$ then $\underline{u}_T - q$ is an UMVU estimator of λ_T whereas $\max(\underline{u}_T - q,0)$ has smaller mean squared error (see e.g. K.M. Lal Saxena and Khurseed Alam (1982), they show that $\max(\underline{u}_T - q,0)$ also dominates the maximum likelihood estimator for λ_T). So both suggestions have some appeal. Since $X\hat{\underline{\beta}}$ is better than $X\underline{b}$ when $\lambda_T < q$ it seems reasonable to decide to use $X\hat{\beta}$ instead of Xb if and only if the estimate of λ_T is less than q. Clearly, $u_T - q < q$ iff $\max(u_T - q,0) < q$, therefore we arrive at the following simple rule:

Estimate the systematic part of $\underline{y}$ *with* $X\hat{\beta}$ *if* $u_T < 2q$, *otherwise use* Xb.

Note that in terms of the 'F'-statistic the condition is $F < 2$. Taking the minimum of Mallows' C-statistics, cf. Mallows (1973), formula (6), and minimizing a form of Akaike's information criterion, cf. Judge et.al. (1980), section 11.5.1, is equivalent to the rule suggested here.

3. CROSS-VALIDATION

The number of 2q crops up also when one uses a certain data-analytic, sample reuse, or cross-validation method to decide which of the two estimates b and $\hat{\beta}$ to choose. For discussions of sample reuse and cross-validation methods, related to the 'leave one out'-methodology, we refer to Ball (1963), Efron (1979, 1982), Geisser (1975), Hocking (1976), Mosteller & Tukey (1977), Stone (1974), the contributions of H. Wold to Jöreskog & Wold (1982), Dijkstra (1981, 1983a,b). Within the context of the present paper, the idea may be described as follows: let (y,X) be given and suppose one decides to use either b'x or $\hat{\beta}'x$, $x \in \mathbb{R}^k$, for conditional prediction purposes. It is obviously desirable to have some information about the quality of both methods. Using the available data one could 'test' both methods T times in the following way. Delete the first row of (y,X) giving $(y_{(1)},X_{(1)})$, say. Calculate $b_{(1)} \equiv (X'_{(1)}X_{(1)})^{-1}X'_{(1)}y_{(1)}$ and predict y_1 with $b'_{(1)}x_1$, yielding a prediction error $y_1 - b'_{(1)}x_1$. Restore the matrix (y,X), delete now the second row and calculate $y_2 - b'_{(2)}x_2$, with an obvious definition of $b_{(2)}$. Repeat this process for t = 1,2,... ...,T. Determine similarly for t = 1,2,...,T $y_t - \hat{\beta}'_{(t)}x_t$. It may be reasonable to decide to use $\hat{\beta}'x$ instead of b'x if and only if Q < 1 with

$$Q \equiv \frac{\sum_1^T (y_t - \hat{\beta}'_{(t)}x_t)^2}{\sum_1^T (y_t - b'_{(t)}x_t)^2} \tag{16}$$

The relation between $\{\underline{Q} < 1\}$ and $\{\underline{u}_T < 2q\}$ is expressed in the statement: If in addition to the assumptions made in section 1 the vectors $(x'_t, z'_t)'$ are uniformly bounded then

$$(T-k)(\underline{Q}-1) - (\underline{u}_T - 2q) \xrightarrow{p} 0 \tag{17}$$

Roughly, if T is sufficiently large, the data-analytic and hypothesis testing approach will lead with high probability to the same decision. For a formal, somewhat lenghty, proof of (17) see Dijkstra (1983b). A heuristic argument for (17) can be sketched as follows:

Let without loss of generality R = (0,I), r = 0 so that the data generating mechanism is

$$\underline{y} = X_1\beta_1^o + X_2\frac{\delta_2}{2\sqrt{T}} + Z\frac{\gamma}{\sqrt{T}} + \underline{\varepsilon} \tag{18}$$

with X_1 of order T×(k−q), $\beta_1^o \in \mathbb{R}^{k-q}$, X_2 is a matrix of order T×q and $\delta_2 \in \mathbb{R}^q$. Then

$$\underline{u}_T = \frac{\underline{e}_1'\underline{e}_1 - \underline{e}'\underline{e}}{\underline{e}'\underline{e}/(T-k)} \tag{19}$$

with $\underline{e} \equiv \underline{y} - X\underline{b}$, $\underline{e}_1 \equiv \underline{y} - X\hat{\underline{\beta}} = \underline{y} - X_1(X_1'X_1)^{-1}X_1'\underline{y}$. Some matrix algebra gives

$$\underline{Q} = \frac{\underline{e}_1'D_1^{-2}\underline{e}_1}{\underline{e}'D^{-2}\underline{e}} \tag{20}$$

with $D \equiv \text{diag}(I - X(X'X)^{-1}X')$, $D_1 \equiv \text{diag}(I - X_1(X_1'X_1)^{-1}X_1')$.

It is easily verified that the diagonal elements of D and D_1 converge to one, uniformly, when $T \to \infty$. Suppose D's diagonal elements are equal so that, since $\operatorname{tr} D = T-k$, $D = \frac{T-k}{T} . I$. And similarly for D_1, $D_1 = \frac{T-k+q}{T} . I$. Then $(T-k)(\underline{Q}-1) - (\underline{u}_T - 2q)$ equals

$$\frac{(\underline{e}_1'\underline{e}_1)/(T-k+q)}{(\underline{e}'\underline{e})/(T-k)} . \left[\frac{(T-k)^2-(T-k+q)^2}{T-k+q}\right] + 2q$$

The random term tends in probability to one, as is easily verified, and the ratio between brackets equals $-2q + q^2/(T-k+q)$ which tends to $-2q$ and (17) 'follows'.

4. PRE-TEST ESTIMATORS

So it appears that the simple 2q-rule can be motivated in various intuitively appealing ways. However, it would be short-sighted to end the story here. For, clearly, the rule defines another estimator $\underline{\hat{\beta}}_2$, say, which belongs to a class of estimators $\{\underline{\hat{\beta}}_c\}$ given by:

$$\underline{\hat{\beta}}_c \equiv \underset{[0,cq)}{I}(\underline{u}_T).\underline{\hat{\beta}} + \underset{[cq,\infty)}{I}(\underline{u}_T).\underline{b} \qquad (21)$$

c is real and nonnegative and $I_A(x) = 1$ if $x \in A$, it is zero otherwise. Estimators like $\underline{\hat{\beta}}_c$ are known as 'pre-test estimators' and there exists a vast literature about the properties of these statistics. A very useful source is a book by Judge & Bock (1978). (Since we will refer to their work frequently we will use the abbreviation J&B in the sequel.) In this book the authors analyse the standard linear model with $\gamma = 0$ and normally distributed residuals. We will extend their results to the asymptotic case, derive the asymptotic distribution of $\sqrt{T}(\underline{\hat{\beta}}_c - \beta_T^*)$, its mean and covariance matrix and also obtain some information about the average squared distance between $X\underline{\hat{\beta}}_c$ and $X\beta_T^*$. In addition we will find some support, using results obtained by Brook (1976), for the statement that c = 2 is approximately an optimal, minimax regret, choice.

We know that $\underline{v}_T \equiv \sqrt{T}(\underline{b} - \beta_T^*)$ tends in law to a random vector $\underline{v}$, say, with $\underline{v} \sim \mathcal{N}(0, \sigma^2 \Sigma_{xx}^{-1})$. Formula (7) can be written in the form

$$\sqrt{T}(\underline{\hat{\beta}} - \beta_T^*) = \mu_T + A_T \underline{v}_T$$

The definition of μ_T and A_T will be clear. It is easily verified that with $\mu \equiv \lim_{T\to\infty} \mu_T$ and $A \equiv \lim_{T\to\infty} A_T$

$$\sqrt{T}(\underline{\hat{\beta}} - \beta_T^*) = \mu + A\underline{v}_T + o_p(1)$$

Also, $\underline{u}_T = (\mu + (A-I)\underline{v}_T)' \frac{\Sigma_{xx}}{\sigma^2} (\mu + (A-I)\underline{v}_T) + o_p(1)$.

Consequently, see e.g. Rao (1973) section 2c.4 (X,XIII), the joint limiting distribution of $[\sqrt{T}(\underline{b}-\beta_T^*)', \sqrt{T}(\hat{\underline{\beta}}-\beta_T^*)', \underline{u}_T]'$ is given by the joint distribution of $[\underline{v}', (\mu+A\underline{v})', \underline{u}]'$ with $\underline{u}$ defined as

$$\underline{u} \equiv (\mu+(A-I)\underline{v})' \frac{\Sigma_{xx}}{\sigma^2} (\mu+(A-I)\underline{v})$$

Formula (21) can be written as

$$\sqrt{T}(\hat{\underline{\beta}}_c-\beta_T^*) = \underset{[0,cq)}{I}(\underline{u}_T).\sqrt{T}(\hat{\underline{\beta}}-\beta_T^*) + \underset{[cq,\infty)}{I}(\underline{u}_T).\sqrt{T}(\underline{b}-\beta_T^*) \quad (22)$$

Since $\sqrt{T}(\hat{\underline{\beta}}_c-\beta_T^*)$ is a continuous function of the statistics appearing in (22), except on a set with limiting zero probability, we may deduce (see Bishop et.al. (1975) p. 472)

$$\sqrt{T}(\hat{\underline{\beta}}_c-\beta_T^*) \xrightarrow{L} \underset{[0,cq)}{I}(\underline{u}).(\mu+A\underline{v}) + \underset{[cq,\infty)}{I}(\underline{u}).\underline{v} \quad (23)$$

Obviously the asymptotic distribution is normal only if $c=0$ or $c=\infty$. As in J&B we can now use theorems derived by Stein and Sclove et.al. (references in J&B, see in particular appendix B) to find e.g. the mean and covariance matrix of $\hat{\underline{\beta}}_c$'s asymptotic distribution. However, there is a short cut, so there is no need to go through lenghty derivations. The asymptotic case as considered here is a simplification of the finite sample situation as analysed by J&B. They had to deal with an additional random variable $\underline{s}^2$ with $(T-k)\underline{s}^2 \sim \sigma^2\chi^2(T-k)$. A close examination of their derivations (J&B ch. 4) easily reveals that all we have to do, apart from making simple notational changes, is to replace $\frac{\chi^2(T-k)}{(T-k)}$ by one wherever it appears. So the mean of the asymptotic distribution of $\sqrt{T}(\hat{\underline{\beta}}_c-\beta_T^*)$ equals

$$-h_\lambda(2).\Sigma_{xx}^{-1}R'(R\Sigma_{xx}^{-1}R')^{-1}R(\delta+\Sigma_{xx}^{-1}\Sigma_{xz}\gamma) = h_\lambda(2).\mu \quad (24)$$

with

$$h_\lambda(j) \equiv \Pr\{\chi^2(q+j,\lambda) < c.q\} \quad (25)$$

(See J&B p. 115, (5.4.3)). And the asymptotic covariance matrix of the pre-test estimator, ascov $\sqrt{T}(\hat{\underline{\beta}}_c-\beta_T^*)$, is given by

$$\begin{aligned}&\text{ascov } \sqrt{T}(\hat{\underline{\beta}}-\beta_T^*) \text{ plus } (1-h_\lambda(2)) \times \{\text{the p.s.d. difference between} \\ &\text{ascov } \sqrt{T}(\underline{b}-\beta_T^*) \text{ and ascov } \sqrt{T}(\hat{\underline{\beta}}-\beta_T^*)\} \text{ plus } \mu\mu' \times \{2h_\lambda(2)-h_\lambda(4)-h_\lambda^2(2)\}\end{aligned} \quad (26)$$

Compare J&B p. 116 (5.4.7). Note that $2h_\lambda(2) - h_\lambda(4) - h_\lambda^2(2)$ is positive because $h_\lambda(4) < h_\lambda(2)$. If $\mu = 0$, then all estimators considered here are unbiased for β_T^*. In addition: ascov $\sqrt{T}(\hat{\underline{\beta}}-\beta_T^*) \leqq$ ascov $\sqrt{T}(\hat{\underline{\beta}}_c-\beta_T^*) \leqq$ ascov $\sqrt{T}(\underline{b}-\beta_T^*)$, where $A \leqq B$ means that $B-A$ is p.s.d.

The first inequality says that testing correct restrictions, $\mu = 0$, has a price (which increases when c decreases). Incidentally, μ and λ may be zero even when δ and γ are not. If $\mu \neq 0$, $\hat{\underline{\beta}}_c$ has smaller absolute bias than $\hat{\underline{\beta}}$. Also for fixed c, $\lambda \to \infty$ implies that ascov $\sqrt{T}(\hat{\underline{\beta}}_c-\beta^*_T) \to$ ascov $\sqrt{T}(\underline{b}-\beta^*_T)$, in fact the unrestricted and pre-test estimator will then have the same asymptotic distribution. Turning now to $\frac{1}{\sigma^2}E(X\hat{\underline{\beta}}_c-X\beta^*_T)'(X\hat{\underline{\beta}}_c-X\beta^*_T) = \frac{1}{\sigma^2}E(\hat{\underline{\beta}}_c-\beta^*_T)'X'X(\hat{\underline{\beta}}_c-\beta^*_T)$ we note that

$$\frac{1}{\sigma^2}\sqrt{T}(\hat{\underline{\beta}}_c-\beta^*_T)'\frac{X'X}{T}\cdot\sqrt{T}(\hat{\underline{\beta}}_c-\beta^*_T) \xrightarrow{L}$$

$$(\underset{[0,cq)}{I}(\underline{u})(\mu+A\underline{v})+\underset{[cq,\infty)}{I}(\underline{u})\cdot\underline{v})'\frac{\Sigma_{xx}}{\sigma^2}(\underset{[0,cq)}{I}(\underline{u})(\mu+A\underline{v})+\underset{[cq,\infty)}{I}(\underline{u})\cdot\underline{v}) \tag{27}$$

From J&B, section (4.7) one obtains that the expectation of the righthand-side of (27) is equal to

$$k-qh_\lambda(2)-\lambda[h_\lambda(4)-2h_\lambda(2)] \tag{28}$$

We will compare (28) with k and $(k-q)+\lambda$, the (asymptotic) average squared error attainable with $\underline{b}$ and $\hat{\underline{\beta}}$ resp. Using J&B, section (4.4) we derive easily:

$$\lambda \leqq \frac{q}{2} \Rightarrow (k-q)+\lambda \leqq (28) \leqq k$$

$$\frac{q}{2} \leqq \lambda \leqq q \Rightarrow (k-q)+\lambda \leqq ((28),k)$$

$$q \leqq \lambda \leqq q/\Pr\{\chi^2(q,0) \geqq c.q\} \Rightarrow k \leqq ((28),(k-q)+\lambda)$$

$$\lambda \geqq q/\Pr\{\chi^2(q,0) \geqq c.q\} \Rightarrow k \leqq (28) \leqq (k-q)+\lambda$$

From the observations made above we have graphically, compare also J&B and Brook (1976) or Wallace & Ashar (1972)

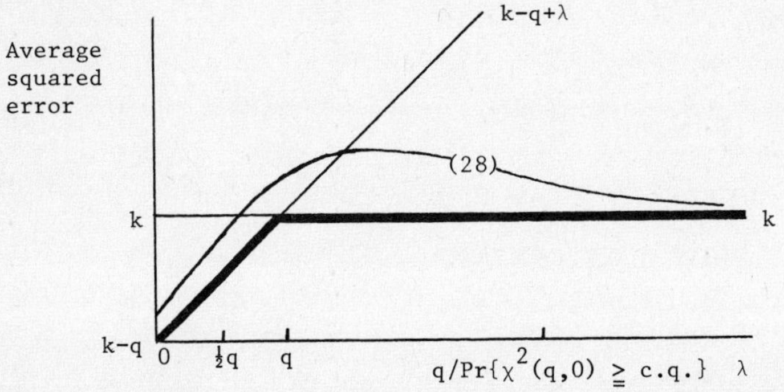

So, the pre-test estimator is at best 'second-best'. Its quality depends on c however and it it natural to try to choose c in such a way that the curved line is 'as close as possible' to the heavy line. Let the 'regret function' be the function whose graph is the vertical distance between the curved and solid line. One reasonable way of defining 'as close as possible', see e.g. Brook (1976), is:

choose c *such that the maximum of the regret function is minimal.*

It is intuitively clear that when c increases the maximum regret on [0,q] decreases whereas it increases on (q,∞). It would follow that the optimal c value, c^*, is such that the maxima are equal. Brook (1976) proved this rigorously for the regret function for the classical linear model (with $\gamma = 0$, normally distributed residuals, and finite T) and his proof is easily adapted to the situation considered here. However it is a non-trivial exercise to calculate c^*. Brook noted for the 35 combinations of q and T-k which he considered that c^* seems to be almost independent of q and T-k: c^* is invariably close to 2. Other criteria seem to lead also to $c^* = 2$, see J&B, section 3.3.3 and Judge et.al. ch. 11. So the simple rule suggested earlier may within the set-up of this paper have some real value.

5. HYPOTHESIS TESTING

In the hypothesis testing tradition one chooses, frequently ignoring power considerations, a certain significance level α, e.g. the celebrated 5%. This level then determines, at least approximately, a critical value obtainable from tables for χ^2-distributions (if no power considerations are involved in the choice of α the critical value appears to be quite arbitrary). The approach proposed in this paper reverses the order: choose a critical value which then determines, approximately, the significance level. The particular choice, 2q, made here is based on the following decisions: 1) set $E\underline{y}$ as the target, 2) measure the performance of the estimators by means of their 'average squared distance' to $E\underline{y}$, and 3) choose the critical value of the test in such a way that the maximum regret for the pre-test estimator, where regret is defined with respect to two specific alternatives, is minimized. Clearly, one could set other targets, take more competitors and choose other scalar or non-scalar quality measures (see e.g. J&B ch. 5). To put it negatively, the arbitrariness of the α level is largely replaced by arbitrary definitions of loss functions, which may or may not be reasonable for problems arising in practice.

The following table gives some large-sample approximations of significance levels α_q defined by

$$\alpha_q \equiv \Pr\{\text{reject } R\beta_o = r \mid \delta=0,\gamma=0\} = \Pr\{\underline{u}_T > 2q \mid \delta=0,\gamma=0\}$$

So $\alpha_q \approx \Pr\{\chi^2(q,0) > 2q\}$

$q =$	1	2	3	4	5	6	7	8	9	10	15	20
$\alpha_q \approx$	15,7%	13,5%	11,2%	9,2%	7,5%	6,2%	5,1%	4,2%	3,5%	2,9%	1,2%	0,5%

Roughly speaking, the more daring the hypothesis (: the larger the reduction of the parameter space), the more tolerant the test becomes. This may be an appealing property.

Finally, we have not considered Stein-rule estimators in this paper, basically for two reasons: 1) their stochastic properties are very difficult to find analytically, 2) the phenomenon which inspired their formulation, see J&B p. 165, seems to be characteristic for continuous distributions, cf. Gutmann (1982); see also Ullah et.al. (1983) who show that (for $\gamma=0$) the conditions under which Stein-rule estimators dominate the simple least squares estimator $\underline{b}$, w.r.t. measures of mean squared error, can be quite sensitive to the assumption of normality. We refer also to Sclove (1968), especially section 3, for some additional problems.

6. THE SIMULTANEOUS SYSTEM

In this and the remaining section we will extend the results obtained to simultaneous, interdependent systems. The derivations will be kept short and sketched only, due to the almost perfect analogy to the case dealt with earlier.

We have available two matrices Y and X of order $T\times l$ and $T\times k$ resp., $T \geqq k$; X is non-stochastic and of full rank. The t-th row of (Y,X) is written as (y_t', x_t'). We assume that for $t = 1,2,\ldots,T$ the y_t's are generated by:

$$B_T \underline{y}_t = \Gamma_T x_t + \Delta_T z_t + \underline{\delta}_t \tag{29}$$

The random $l\times 1$ vectors $\underline{\delta}_t$ are i.i.d. with zero mean and p.d. covariance matrix $\Sigma_{\delta\delta}$; z_t' is the t-th row of a $T\times m$ non-stochastic matrix Z; the assumption concerning the convergence of the moment matrices $\frac{1}{T}X'X$, $\frac{1}{T}X'Z$, $\frac{1}{T}Z'Z$, equation (2), is adopted here also.

In addition we have:

$$(B_T, \Gamma_T, \Delta_T) = (B_o + \frac{1}{\sqrt{T}} D_b, \Gamma_o + \frac{1}{\sqrt{T}} D_c, \frac{1}{\sqrt{T}} \Delta) \tag{30}$$

Both B_T and B_o are non-singular $l\times l$ matrices with unit diagonal; D_b is also of order $l\times l$; Γ_T, Γ_o, D_c are $l\times k$ matrices, Δ_T and Δ are of order $l\times m$. The pair (B_o, Γ_o) belongs to a class of matrices satisfying certain restrictions which, for simplicity, take here the form of specifying the position of zero entries. We assume that no other pair (B,Γ) with the same prescribed zero entries and $\operatorname{diag} B = I$ has the property that $B^{-1}\Gamma = \Pi_o \equiv B_o^{-1}\Gamma_o$. Concerning $\Sigma_{\delta\delta}$, no specific assumptions are made other then symmetry and positive definiteness. For further reference we define the

non-negative number q as the difference between kl and the number of elements in (B_o,Γ_o) which are not a priori specified to be either zero or one.
From (29) it follows that

$$\underline{y}_t = B_T^{-1}\Gamma_T x_t + B_T^{-1}\Delta_T z_t + B_T^{-1}\underline{\delta}_t \tag{31}$$

So $\underline{Y} = X\Gamma_T' B_T'^{-1} + Z\Delta_T' B_T'^{-1}$ + residuals.
Suppose as before that a researcher unaware of the existence or relevance of Z is interested in estimating the systematic part of $\underline{Y}$ as well as possible. It is easily verified that the conditional expectation of each column of $\underline{Y}$ is best approximated (in a least squares sense) using X only by X times the corresponding column of $(\Pi_T^*)'$ with

$$\Pi_T^* \equiv B_T^{-1}\Gamma_T + B_T^{-1}\Delta_T Z'X(X'X)^{-1} \tag{32}$$

Consider now the unrestricted regression matrix $\underline{P}$ defined by

$$\underline{P} \equiv \sum_1^T \underline{y}_t x_t' . (\sum_1^T x_t x_t')^{-1} = Y'X(X'X)^{-1} \tag{33}$$

$$\text{Clearly, } \underline{P} = \Pi_T^* + B_T^{-1} . \sum_1^T \underline{\delta}_t x_t' . (\sum_1^T x_t x_t')^{-1} \tag{34}$$

Consequently, the mean of $\text{vec}(\underline{P}-\Pi_T^*)'$ equals zero, its covariance matrix is simply, with $\Sigma_T \equiv B_T^{-1}\Sigma_{\delta\delta}B_T'^{-1}$,

$$\Sigma_T \otimes (X'X)^{-1} \tag{35}$$

We also have

$$\sqrt{T}\, \text{vec}(\underline{P}-\Pi_T^*)' \xrightarrow{L} \mathcal{N}(0,\Sigma\otimes\Sigma_{xx}^{-1}) \tag{36}$$

with $\Sigma \equiv \lim \Sigma_T = B_o^{-1}\Sigma_{\delta\delta}B_o'^{-1}$, as is easily checked.
It seems reasonable to measure the quality of $X\underline{P}'$ by means of the following straightforward extension of the measure employed in the preceding sections:

$$E\, \text{vec}'[X(\underline{P}-\Pi_T^*)'](\Sigma_T^{-1}\otimes I)\text{vec}[X(\underline{P}-\Pi_T^*)'] \tag{37}$$

which can also be written as

$$E\, \text{vec}'(\underline{P}-\Pi_T^*)'(\Sigma_T^{-1}\otimes(X'X))\text{vec}(\underline{P}-\Pi_T^*)' \tag{38}$$

or

$$\text{tr}\{(\Sigma_T^{-1}\otimes(X'X).E\, \text{vec}(\underline{P}-\Pi_T^*)'\text{vec}'(P-\Pi_T^*)'\} \tag{39}$$

Again, when comparing the estimators it is irrelevant whether we measure the distance to vec $X(\Pi_T^*)'$ or to vec $E\underline{Y}$.
Combining (39) with (35) yields immediately that the average squared error as defined

here is equal to kl, the number of elements of $\underline{P}$.

Alternatively, one could decide to use $\hat{\Pi}$ instead of P, where $\hat{\Pi} \equiv \hat{B}^{-1}\hat{\Gamma}$ and the pair $(\hat{B},\hat{\Gamma})$ minimizes a suitably chosen fitting function over the set of $l\times(l+k)$ matrices (B,Γ) having the same prescribed zero and one entries as (B_o,Γ_o). I.e. one could adopt the working hypothesis that 'the model is correct' (: $(D_b,D_c,\Delta) = 0$). Define

$$S \equiv \frac{1}{T}\sum_{1}^{T}(y_t-Px_t)(y_t-Px_t)' \tag{40}$$

Some possible fitting functions are

$$\text{vec}'(P-B^{-1}\Gamma)(\frac{X'X}{T}\otimes S^{-1})\text{vec}(P-B^{-1}\Gamma) \tag{41}$$

$$|I+S^{-1}(P-B^{-1}\Gamma)\frac{X'X}{T}(P-B^{-1}\Gamma)'| \tag{42}$$

or, with $\underline{W} \overset{P}{\to} \Sigma_{\delta\delta}^{-1}$

$$\text{vec}'(BP-\Gamma)(\frac{X'X}{T}\otimes W)\text{vec}(BP-\Gamma) \tag{43}$$

The first and third fitting function are based on generalized least squares theory, minimization of (43) leads to 3SLS estimates; minimizing (42) is the same as maximizing the likelihood function based on the working hypothesis of normality of $\underline{\delta}_t$. It does not really matter, at least asymptotically, which of the three functions one chooses: the estimators are asymptotically equivalent. This fact is easily proved: use the implicit function theorem to express the appropriately normalized estimators as linear functions of $\sqrt{T}\,\text{vec}(\underline{P}-\Pi_T^*)'$ plus $o_p(1)$ and check that each fitting function defines the same linear function. The main burden of the proof is carried by differentiation of the fitting functions w.r.t. the elements of (B,Γ), twice, and w.r.t. (B,Γ) followed by differentiation w.r.t. vec P'. In the sequel we will focus on (43), 3SLS, since it is the simplest function. (See also Bentler & Dijkstra (1983). Reasons for not using 2SLS or 'direct least squares on the structural form' will be given below.

In section 7 we prove a number of statements including

1. $\sqrt{T}\,\text{vec}(\underline{\hat{\Pi}}-\Pi_T^*)'$ is asymptotically normally distributed with mean μ, say.
2. $\text{vec}'(\underline{\hat{\Pi}}-\Pi_T^*)'(\Sigma_T^{-1}\otimes(X'X)).\text{vec}(\underline{\hat{\Pi}}-\Pi_T^*)'$, compare (38), tends in law to a distribution with mean kl-q plus a non-negative number λ.
3. let $\underline{W}$ be an estimator for $\Sigma_{\delta\delta}^{-1}$ based on 2SLS, then $\underline{\hat{B}}'\underline{W}\underline{\hat{B}} \overset{P}{\to} \Sigma^{-1}$; moreover, T times (43) evaluated at $(\underline{\hat{B}},\underline{\hat{\Gamma}})$ equals $\underline{u}_T$, say, with
$\underline{u}_T \equiv \sqrt{T}\,\text{vec}'(\underline{P}-\underline{\hat{\Pi}})'((\underline{\hat{B}}'\underline{W}\underline{\hat{B}})\otimes(\frac{X'X}{T})).\sqrt{T}\,\text{vec}(P-\hat{\Pi})' \overset{L}{\to} \chi^2(q,\lambda)$.
As before this suggests the rule: use $X\hat{\Pi}'$ instead of XP' iff $u_T < 2q$.

In addition we have parallel results for the pre-test estimator $\underline{\hat{\Pi}}_c$ defined by

$$\underline{\hat{\Pi}}_c \equiv \underset{[0,cq)}{I(\underline{u}_T)}\,.\,\underline{\hat{\Pi}} + \underset{[cq,\infty)}{I(\underline{u}_T)}\,.\,\underline{P}$$

4. the asymptotic distribution of $\sqrt{T}\,\mathrm{vec}(\hat{\underline{\Pi}}_c-\Pi^*_T)'$ has mean $h_\lambda(2).\mu$, with $h_\lambda(j) \equiv$ $\equiv \Pr\{\chi^2(q+j,\lambda) < c.q\}$; its covariance matrix, $\mathrm{ascov}\sqrt{T}\,\mathrm{vec}(\hat{\underline{\Pi}}_c-\Pi^*_T)'$ is given by: $\mathrm{ascov}\sqrt{T}\,\mathrm{vec}(\hat{\underline{\Pi}}-\Pi^*_T)'$ plus $(1-h_\lambda(2)) \times$ {the p.s.d. difference between $\mathrm{ascov}\sqrt{T}\,\mathrm{vec}\,(\underline{P}-\Pi^*_T)'$ and $\mathrm{ascov}\sqrt{T}\,\mathrm{vec}(\hat{\underline{\Pi}}-\Pi^*_T)'$} plus $\mu\mu' \times \{2h_\lambda(2)-h_\lambda(4)-h^2_\lambda(2)\}$.
5. $\mathrm{vec}'(\hat{\underline{\Pi}}_c-\Pi^*_T)'(\Sigma_T^{-1}\otimes(X'X))\mathrm{vec}(\hat{\underline{\Pi}}_c-\Pi^*_T)'$ tends in law to a random variable with mean $kl-qh_\lambda(2)-\lambda[h_\lambda(4)-2h_\lambda(2)]$.

Again, we have that c = 2 will be in sufficiently large samples an approximately optimal (minimax regret) choice. So the results are very similar to those found for the one-equation linear model.

We close this section with some remarks. First, we expect that the results obtained may be extended to stable dynamic systems, since the derivations depend heavily on the fact expressed in (36), and (36) is valid also for (correctly specified) stable dynamic systems, see Theil (1971) ch. 10 (x_t now stands for predetermined variables). In addition, sufficiently smooth non-linear systems may be covered as well, perhaps along the lines of Sen (1979).

Second, we have refrained from analyzing 2SLS and OLS, 'least squares on the structural form', for the following reasons. Some Monte Carlo experiments for correctly specified small systems with normal distributions, see e.g. Summers (1965) and Mosbaek & Wold (1970), indicate that 2SLS reduced form estimators do not outperform $\underline{P}$, neither with regard to estimation nor with regard to prediction. The same is true for OLS. In addition, it appears that with respect to estimation of the reduced form and prediction, 'full-information' methods are preferable to 2SLS and OLS; see e.g. Raj (1980) whose small system experiments also indicate that the ranking is invariant w.r.t. the residual-distribution. Summer's (1965) Monte Carlo study shows that the ranking may be maintained even when the model is misspecified. Dhrymes (1973) has shown that generally there is no guarantee that $\underline{P}$ is outperformed by the 2SLS-estimator (as opposed to full-information methods), i.e. the difference between the asymptotic covariance matrices is indeterminate. As a final observation: the robustness of 2SLS and OLS against misspecification clearly offers some comfort only when one focuses on structural form parameters, and not when the reduced form is of main interest.

7. PROOFS

Let the $(kl-q)\times 1$ vector θ be obtained by stacking vec B' and vec Γ' with all elements deleted which are a priori equal to zero or one. Let θ_o be the corresponding vector for (B_o,Γ_o). We will write $2.F(\theta\mid P,W,\frac{X'X}{T})$ for the fitting function defined in (43).

From (30) and (32) one obtains, neglecting o(1) terms:

$$\sqrt{T}\ \mathrm{vec}(\Pi_T^*-\Pi_o)' = [-B_o^{-1}\otimes \Pi_o', B_o^{-1}\otimes I]\begin{bmatrix}\mathrm{vec}\ D_b' \\ \mathrm{vec}\ D_c'\end{bmatrix} + \mathrm{vec}(\Sigma_{xx}^{-1}\Sigma_{xz}\Delta' B_o'^{-1}) \tag{44}$$

The righthand-side of (44) will be denoted by d. Formula (36) implies:

$$\sqrt{T}\ \mathrm{vec}(\underline{P}-\Pi_o)' \overset{L}{\to} \mathcal{N}(d, \Sigma\otimes\Sigma_{xx}^{-1}) \tag{45}$$

Evidently, $\underline{P} \overset{p}{\to} \Pi_o$. Using the identifiability of (B_o,Γ_o) it is easy to prove that F is *strictly* convex in θ for all $(P,W,\frac{X'X}{T})$ in an open set containing $(\Pi_o,\Sigma_{\delta\delta}^{-1},\Sigma_{xx})$, with W and $\frac{X'X}{T}$ p.d. In what follows we will limit the discussion to this set. Because of the strict convexity and differentiability of F we know that $F(\theta|P,W,\frac{X'X}{T})$ attains a global minimum in the unique point $\hat{\theta} = \hat{\theta}(P,W,\frac{X'X}{T})$ solvable from $\frac{\partial F}{\partial\theta} = 0$. The derivatives are:

$$\frac{\partial F}{\partial\theta} = \begin{bmatrix} I\otimes P \\ -I\end{bmatrix}(W\otimes\frac{1}{T}X'X)[I\otimes P', -I]\begin{bmatrix}\mathrm{vec}\ B' \\ \mathrm{vec}\ \Gamma'\end{bmatrix} =$$

$$\begin{bmatrix} W\otimes\frac{Y'X}{T}(\frac{X'X}{T})^{-1}\frac{X'Y}{T} & -W\otimes\frac{1}{T}Y'X \\ -W\otimes\frac{1}{T}X'Y & W\otimes\frac{1}{T}X'X\end{bmatrix}\begin{bmatrix}\mathrm{vec}\ B' \\ \mathrm{vec}\ \Gamma'\end{bmatrix} \tag{46}$$

Or more compactly

$$\frac{\partial F}{\partial\theta} = \begin{bmatrix}\mathrm{vec}(P\frac{X'X}{T}(P'B'-\Gamma')W) \\ -\mathrm{vec}(\frac{X'X}{T}(P'B'-\Gamma')W)\end{bmatrix}$$

where it is to be understood that rows corresponding to fixed elements of (B,Γ) are deleted.

Note that the matrix of second order derivatives, $\frac{\partial^2 F}{\partial\theta\partial\theta'}$, is just the matrix of (46) with columns corresponding to fixed elements deleted. Due to the uniqueness of $\hat{\theta}$ this Hessian has a non-zero determinant, in fact it is p.d. everywhere. Obviously, $\underline{\hat{\theta}} \overset{p}{\to} \theta_o$. It is also clear that $\hat{\theta}$ is a continuously differentiable function of its arguments in a neighbourhood of $(\Pi_o,\Sigma_{\delta\delta}^{-1},\Sigma_{xx})$. Observe that $\hat{\theta}(\Pi_o,W,\frac{X'X}{T}) = \theta_o$ for all $(W,\frac{X'X}{T})$. Consequently

$$\sqrt{T}(\hat{\theta}-\theta_o) = -(\frac{\partial^2 F}{\partial\theta\partial\theta'})^{-1}\frac{\partial^2 F}{\partial\theta\partial\mathrm{vec}'P'}\cdot\sqrt{T}\ \mathrm{vec}(P-\Pi_o)' \tag{47}$$

where each row of the matrix product of derivatives is evaluated at a point, depending on $(W,\frac{X'X}{T})$, on the line segment connecting vec P' and vec Π_o'. Note that

$$\frac{\partial^2 F}{\partial\theta\partial \text{vec}'P'} = \begin{bmatrix} K_{lk}((WBP\frac{X'X}{T}\otimes I)-(W\Gamma\frac{X'X}{T}\otimes I))+(WB\otimes P\frac{X'X}{T}) \\ -WB\otimes\frac{X'X}{T} \end{bmatrix} \tag{48}$$

with K_{lk} defined by vec P' = K_{lk} vec P (see Magnus & Neudecker (1979) for properties of K_{lk}), and of course rows corresponding to fixed elements of (B,Γ) are deleted. In the sequel we will let $\frac{\partial^2F^o}{\partial\theta\partial\theta'}$ and $\frac{\partial^2F^o}{\partial\theta\partial \text{vec}'P'}$ stand for the probability limits of the matrices of derivatives. So

$$\frac{\partial^2F^o}{\partial\theta\partial\theta'} = \begin{bmatrix} \Sigma_{\delta\delta}^{-1}\otimes\Pi_o\Sigma_{xx}\Pi_o' & -\Sigma_{\delta\delta}^{-1}\otimes\Pi_o\Sigma_{xx} \\ -\Sigma_{\delta\delta}^{-1}\otimes\Sigma_{xx}\Pi_o' & \Sigma_{\delta\delta}^{-1}\otimes\Sigma_{xx} \end{bmatrix} \tag{49}$$

and

$$\frac{\partial^2F^o}{\partial\theta\partial \text{vec}'P'} = \begin{bmatrix} \Sigma_{\delta\delta}^{-1}B_o\otimes\Pi_o\Sigma_{xx} \\ -\Sigma_{\delta\delta}^{-1}B_o\otimes\Sigma_{xx} \end{bmatrix} \tag{50}$$

From (47) we get

$$\sqrt{T}(\underline{\hat\theta}-\theta_o) = -\left(\frac{\partial^2F^o}{\partial\theta\partial\theta'}\right)^{-1}\frac{\partial^2F^o}{\partial\theta\partial \text{vec}'P'}\cdot\sqrt{T}\,\text{vec}\,(\underline{P}-\Pi_o)' + o_p(1) \tag{51}$$

The asymptotic covariance matrix of $\sqrt{T}\,\text{vec}\,(\underline{P}-\Pi_o)'$ equals $\Sigma\otimes\Sigma_{xx}^{-1}$ and it is easily verified that

$$\frac{\partial^2F^o}{\partial\theta\partial \text{vec}'P'}(\Sigma\otimes\Sigma_{xx}^{-1})\left(\frac{\partial^2F^o}{\partial\theta\partial \text{vec}'P'}\right)' = \frac{\partial^2F^o}{\partial\theta\partial\theta'} \tag{52}$$

Consequently,

$$\sqrt{T}(\underline{\hat\theta}-\theta_o) \xrightarrow{L} \mathcal{N}\left(-\left(\frac{\partial^2F^o}{\partial\theta\partial\theta'}\right)^{-1}\frac{\partial^2F^o}{\partial\theta\partial \text{vec}'P'}\cdot d, \left(\frac{\partial^2F^o}{\partial\theta\partial\theta'}\right)^{-1}\right) \tag{53}$$

Finally, we have, since $\sqrt{T}\,\text{vec}\,(\underline{\hat\Pi}-\Pi_o)' = \frac{\partial\text{vec}\Pi'}{\partial\theta_o'}\cdot\sqrt{T}(\underline{\hat\theta}-\theta_o) + o_p(1)$ where $\frac{\partial\text{vec}\Pi'}{\partial\theta_o'}$ is the matrix in (44) with the usual columns deleted,

$$\begin{aligned}\sqrt{T}\,\text{vec}\,(\underline{\hat\Pi}-\Pi_T^*)' &= \left[-\frac{\partial\text{vec}\Pi'}{\partial\theta_o'}\left(\frac{\partial^2F^o}{\partial\theta\partial\theta'}\right)^{-1}\frac{\partial^2F^o}{\partial\theta\partial \text{vec}'P'} - I\right]d \\ &\quad - \frac{\partial\text{vec}\Pi'}{\partial\theta_o'}\left(\frac{\partial^2F^o}{\partial\theta\partial\theta'}\right)^{-1}\frac{\partial^2F^o}{\partial\theta\partial \text{vec}'P'}\cdot\sqrt{T}\,\text{vec}\,(\underline{P}-\Pi_T^*)' + o_p(1)\end{aligned} \tag{54}$$

With this equation the asymptotic distribution of $\sqrt{T}\,\text{vec}\,(\underline{\hat\Pi}-\Pi_T^*)'$ is easily found and statement 1 of section 6 is proved. The definition of μ, the 'asymptotic bias' of $\sqrt{T}\,\text{vec}\,(\underline{\hat\Pi}-\Pi_T^*)'$, will be clear. We will briefly indicate how the validity of the remaining statements can be verified.

The first part of statement 2 is trivial, and the mean of the asymptotic distribution equals:

$$\mathrm{tr}\{\frac{\partial \mathrm{vec}\Pi'}{\partial\theta_o'}(\frac{\partial^2 F^o}{\partial\theta\partial\theta'})^{-1}(\frac{\partial \mathrm{vec}\Pi'}{\partial\theta_o'})'(\Sigma^{-1}\otimes\Sigma_{xx})\} + \mu'(\Sigma^{-1}\otimes\Sigma_{xx})\mu;$$

Since $(\frac{\partial \mathrm{vec}\Pi'}{\partial\theta_o'})'(\Sigma^{-1}\otimes\Sigma_{xx})\frac{\partial \mathrm{vec}\Pi'}{\partial\theta_o'} = \frac{\partial^2 F^o}{\partial\theta\partial\theta'}$ the first term is equal to kl-q and we define

$$\lambda \equiv \mu'(\Sigma^{-1}\otimes\Sigma_{xx})\mu \tag{55}$$

Statement 3 is a bit more involved. The argument leading to the 'consistency' and asymptotic normality of $\hat{\underline{\theta}}$ can be repeated for 2SLS estimators, simply take W = I. The first part of the statement then follows easily. For the second part, note that the asymptotic distribution of $\underline{u}_T$ is the same as the limiting distribution of

$$\sqrt{T}\,\mathrm{vec}'(\underline{\hat{\Pi}}-\underline{P})'(\Sigma^{-1}\otimes\Sigma_{xx}).\sqrt{T}\,\mathrm{vec}(\underline{\hat{\Pi}}-\underline{P})' \tag{56}$$

We now invoke a theorem which can easily be deduced from theorem 9.2.1 of Rao & Mitra (1971): Let $\underline{y}\sim\mathcal{N}(\mu,V)$ where V need not to be regular; let A be some non-random matrix of appropriate order. If VAV = V and $\mu'AVA\mu = \mu'A\mu$ then $\underline{y}'A\underline{y}\sim$ $\sim\chi^2(\mathrm{tr}AV,\mu'A\mu)$. Formulae (54) and (36) yield the asymptotic distribution of $\sqrt{T}\,\mathrm{vec}(\underline{\hat{\Pi}}-\underline{P})'$ and after some tedious matrix algebra one finds that $\underline{u}_T \overset{L}{\to} \chi^2(q,\lambda)$. The asymptotic distribution of the pre-test estimators can now be found using the same arguments as in section 4: let $\underline{v}_T \equiv \sqrt{T}\,\mathrm{vec}(\underline{P}-\Pi_T^*)'$, so $\underline{v}_T \overset{L}{\to} \underline{v}$ whose distribution is given in (36); we can write, compare (54), $\sqrt{T}\,\mathrm{vec}(\underline{\hat{\Pi}}-\Pi_T^*)' = \mu + A\underline{v}_T + o_p(1)$ and $\underline{u}_T$ equals

$$(\mu+(A-I)\underline{v}_T)'(\Sigma^{-1}\otimes\Sigma_{xx})(\mu+(A-I)\underline{v}_T) + o_p(1)$$

$$\overset{L}{\to} \underline{u} \equiv (\mu+(A-I)\underline{v})'(\Sigma^{-1}\otimes\Sigma_{xx})(\mu+(A-I)\underline{v}) \sim \chi^2(q,\lambda)$$

So as before we have

$$\sqrt{T}\,\mathrm{vec}(\underline{\hat{\Pi}}_c-\Pi_T^*)' \overset{L}{\to} \underset{[0,cq)}{I(\underline{u})}\;(\mu+A\underline{v}) + \underset{[cq,\infty)}{I(\underline{u})}\;.\underline{v}$$

The validity of the last two statements is most easily seen when $\hat{\underline{\beta}}$, the restricted least squares estimator, is written in a form matching $\mathrm{vec}(\underline{\hat{\Pi}}')$. First observe that $\{\beta\colon R\beta = 0\} = \{\beta\colon \beta = C\tau\}$ where $\tau\in\mathbb{R}^{k-q}$ and C is a k×(k-q) matrix of rank (k-q) whose columns span the kernel of R. Then minimizing $(b-C\tau)'X'X(b-C\tau)$ yields $\hat{\beta} = C\hat{\tau} = C(C'X'XC)^{-1}C'X'Xb$ so that with a little algebra

$$\sqrt{T}(\underline{\hat{\beta}}-\beta_T^*) = (C(C'\Sigma_{xx}C)^{-1}C'\Sigma_{xx}-I)(\delta+\Sigma_{xx}^{-1}\Sigma_{xz}\gamma) + C(C'\Sigma_{xx}C)^{-1}C'\Sigma_{xx}\sqrt{T}(\underline{b}-\beta_T^*) + o_p(1)$$

where $\delta + \Sigma_{xx}^{-1}\Sigma_{xz}\gamma = \lim_{T\to\infty}\sqrt{T}(\beta_T^* - \beta_o)$.

Clearly, $\frac{\partial vec\Pi'}{\partial\theta_o'}$ matches C, (49) corresponds with $(C'\Sigma_{xx}C)$ and (50) with $-C'\Sigma_{xx}$, etc. Consequently, the results obtained for the linear regression model carry over to simultaneous systems of equations.

One final remark is in order. The expression given for the mean and covariance matrix appear to be difficult to use in practice. We suggest to consider the Bootstrap, a Monte Carlo method based on the empirical distribution of the data; basic references are Efron (1979, 1982). There does not appear to be an abundance of alternatives.

REFERENCES

Ball, R.J. (1963): The significance of simultaneous methods of parameter estimation in econometric models, Applied Statistics 12, 14-25.

Bentler, P.M. and T.K. Dijkstra (1983): Efficient estimation via linearization in structural models, to appear in P.R. Krishnaiah (ed.): Multivariate Analysis VI, (1984) North-Holland, Amsterdam.

Bishop, Y.M.M., S.E. Fienberg and P.W. Holland (1975): Discrete Multivariate Analysis, MIT Press Cambridge, Massachusetts.

Brook, R.J. (1976): On the use of a regret function to set significance points in prior tests of estimation, Journal of the American Statistical Association, 71, 126-131.

Dhrymes, P.J. (1973): Restricted and Unrestricted Reduced Forms: Asymptotic Distribution and Relative Efficiency, Econometrica, 41, 119-134.

Dhrymes, P.J. (1978): Introductory Econometrics, Springer-Verlag, New York.

Dijkstra, T.K. (1981): Latent variables in linear stochastic models, unpublished Ph.D thesis, University of Groningen, Institute of Econometrics.

Dijkstra, T.K. (1983a): Some comments on maximum likelihood and partial least squares methods, Journal of Econometrics, 22, 67-90.

Dijkstra, T.K. (1983b): Predictive tests, Technical report, University of Groningen, Institute of Econometrics.

Efron, B. (1979): Bootstrap methods, another look at the Jackknife, The Annals of Statistics, 7, 1-26.

Efron, B. (1982): The Jackknife, the Bootstrap and other resampling plans, SIAM, Philadelphia.

Fix, E., J.L. Hodges jr. and E.L. Lehman (1959): The restricted chi-square test, pages 92-107 in Probability and Statistics, The Harald Cramér Volume ed. by U. Grenander, John Wiley, New York.

Geisser, S. (1975): The predictive sample reuse method with applications, Journal of the American Statistical Association, 70, 320-328.

Gutmann, S. (1982): Stein's paradox is impossible in problems with finite sample space, The Annals of Statistics, 10, 1017-1020.

Hocking, R.R. (1976): The analysis and selection of variables in linear regression, Biometrics, 32, 1-49.

Jöreskog, K.G. and H. Wold, editors (1982): Systems under indirect observation; Causality-Structure-Prediction, part II, North-Holland, Amsterdam.

Judge, G.G. and M.E. Bock (1978): The Statistical Implications of Pre-Test and Stein-Rule estimators in Econometrics, North-Holland, Amsterdam.

Judge, G.G., W.E. Griffiths, R. Carter Hill and Tsoung-Chao Lee (1980): The theory and practice of econometrics, John Wiley, New York.

Lal Saxena, K.M. and Khurseed Alam (1982): Estimation of the non-centrality parameter of a chi-squared distribution, Annals of Statistics, 10, 1012-1017.

Lehmann, E.L. (1983): Theory of Point Estimation, John Wiley, New York.

Magnus, J.R. and H. Neudecker (1979): The commutation matrix: some properties and applications, The Annals of Statistics, 2, 381-394.
Malinvaud, E. (1970): Statistical methods of econometrics, North-Holland, Amsterdam.
Mallows, C.L. (1973): Some comments on C_p, Technometrics, 15, 661-675.
Mosbaek, E.J. and H. Wold (1970): Interdependent systems: structure and estimation, North-Holland, Amsterdam.
Mosteller, F. and J.W. Tukey (1977): Data analysis and regression: A second course in statistics, Addison-Wesley, Massachusetts.
Raj, B. (1980): A Monte Carlo Study of small-sample properties of simultaneous equation estimators with normal and nonnormal disturbances, Journal of the American Statistical Association, 75, 221-229.
Rao, C.R. and S.K. Mitra (1971): Generalized Inverse of Matrices and its Applications, John Wiley, New York.
Rao, C.R. (1973): Linear Statistical Inference and its Applications, John Wiley, New York.
Sclove, S.L. (1968): Improved estimators for coefficients in linear regression, Journal of the American Statistical Association, 63, 597-606.
Sen, P.K. (1979): Asymptotic properties of maximum likelihood estimators based on conditional specification, The Annals of Statistics, 7, 1019-1033.
Stone, M. (1974): Cross-validatory Choice and Assessment of Statistical Predictions (with discussion), Journal of the Royal Statistical Society, 36, 111-147.
Stroud, T.W.F. (1971): On obtaining large-sample tests from asymptotically normal estimators, Annals of Mathematical Statistics, 42, 1412-1424.
Summers, A. (1965): A capital intensive approach to the small sample properties of various simultaneous equation estimators, Econometrica, 33, 1-41.
Theil, H. (1971): Principles of Econometrics, John Wiley, New York.
Ullah, A. V.K. Srivastava and R. Chandra (1983): Properties of shrinkage estimators in linear regression when disturbances are not normal, Journal of Econometrics, 21, 389-402.
Wallace, T.D. and V.G. Ashar (1972): Sequential methods in model construction, The Review of Economics and Statistics, 14, 172-178.

Added in proof.

Instead of using *either* $\hat{\Pi}$ *or* P one might consider $w\hat{\Pi} + (1-w)P$ for some scalar w. Suppose λ is known. Then the risk, the asymptotic average squared error of $X[w\underline{\hat{\Pi}}+(1-w)\underline{P}]'$, equals $w^2[q+\lambda] - 2wq + kl$ which is minimal for $w = w^* \equiv q/(q+\lambda)$. The estimator $X[w^*\underline{\hat{\Pi}}+(1-w^*)\underline{P}]'$ is better than the best of $X\underline{\hat{\Pi}}'$ and $X\underline{P}'$, except when $\lambda = 0$, in which case it equals $X\underline{\hat{\Pi}}'$. The pre-test estimator, $X\underline{\hat{\Pi}}_c'$, is a fortiori outperformed for *all* values of λ. When λ is unknown one could estimate w^* by $\underline{w} = q/(q+\max(\underline{u}_T-q,0))$. The properties of $X[\underline{w}\underline{\hat{\Pi}}+(1-\underline{w})\underline{P}]'$ remain to be ascertained.

DISCRETE NORMAL LINEAR REGRESSION MODELS

Jan de Leeuw
Department of Data Theory
University of Leiden
Middelstegracht 4, 2312 TW Leiden
The Netherlands

0. ABSTRACT

In this paper we continue our study of the Pearsonian approach to discrete multivariate analysis, in which structural properties of the multivariate normal distribution are combined with the essential discreteness of the data into a single comprehensive model. In an earlier publication we studied these 'block-multinormal' methods for covariance models. Here we propose a similar approach for the regression model with fixed regressors. Likelihood methods are derived and applied to some examples. We review the related literature and point out some interesting possible generalizations. The effect of continuous misspecification of a discrete model is studied in some detail. Relationships with the optimal scaling approach to multivariate analysis are also investigated.

1. INTRODUCTION

In this paper we are interested in various generalizations of the familiar normal linear regression model. These generalizations are intended to be more realistic, at least in most social science situations that we are familiar with, than the classical model. Our starting point is that observed variables are inherently discrete (cf also De Leeuw, 1983). This is true, of course, for both dependent and independent variables, but only the discreteness of the dependent variables has far-reaching consequences for the regression model.

Although observed variables are always discrete, continuous variables can be used in regression modelling for at least two purposes. In the first place the model can stipulate that we are really interested in the relationship between unobservable 'true' continuous variables, of which we have observed discreticized versions. This is the *Pearsonian approach* to discrete variables in multivariate analysis. It is also known as the *treshold approach*, or the *grouped continuous approach*. General discussions and criticisms of this approach, as well as alternatives to this approach, are given in Fienberg (1980), De Leeuw (1983), Winship and Mare (1983), Anderson (1984). Although *Yulean* alternatives (i.e. based on the work of G. Udny Yule) to discrete multivariate analysis are sometimes undoubtedly more natural, we shall restrict our attention in this paper to grouped continuous models. Continuous variables can, in the second place, also be used for computational purposes. A statistical model for a discrete observed phenomenon may be computationally too demanding. In such cases we often approximate the discrete model by a continuous one to simplify the computations. In fact, this is the way the normal distribution originally appeared on the statistical scene. Thus continuous variables have the dual role of modelling the latent or underlying process, and of serving as computational tools.

In this paper we shall study the question in how far such continuous approximations, in our case the classical linear regression estimates, continue to function well in more general discrete models. For completeness we also review and/or derive 'optimal' statistical procedures for discrete regression models. We use the convention of underlining random variables (Hemelrijk, 1966). The abbreviation i.i.d. is used for 'independent and identically distributed'. The notation $\underline{x} \sim N(\mu,\sigma^2)$ is short for 'random variable $\underline{x}$ has a univariate normal distribution with mean μ and variance σ^2'.

2. MODELS

The classical normal linear regression model makes the following assumptions about the sequence of random variables $\underline{y}_i$ (i=1,2,...).

$$\underline{y}_i = x_i'\beta + \underline{\varepsilon}_i. \tag{1a}$$

$$\underline{\varepsilon}_i \text{ i.i.d.} \tag{1b}$$

$$\underline{\varepsilon}_i \sim N(0,\sigma^2). \tag{1c}$$

In (1a) the x_i is a sequence of fixed vectors, say with m elements. The parameters in model (1), which must be estimated, are the m elements of β and the single additional parameter σ^2. Statistical theory for model (1) is entirely routine.

The first generalization we discuss is the *discrete normal linear regression model*. It supposes that the classical model (1) is true for unobserved variables $\underline{y}_i$, which are then discreticized or rounded to produce the observed $\underline{z}_i$. We define the model by four assumptions (2a)-(2d). Assumptions (2a), (2b), and (2c) are the same as (1a), (1b), and (1c). The remaining assumption is

$$\underline{z}_i = \phi(\underline{y}_i), \text{ with } \phi \text{ a monotone step-function.} \tag{2d}$$

In model (2) we assume the number of steps of the step-function to be known. This is entirely natural, because the number of steps is equal to the number of possible values of our discrete observed variable. We also assume, and this is less natural, that the location of the steps are known. Thus there are t known real numbers $\alpha_1 < \alpha_2 < \ldots < \alpha_t$ such that (2d) can also be written as: $\underline{z}_i = s$ if $\alpha_{s-1} < \underline{y}_i \leq \alpha_s$. Here $s \leq t + 1$, and we have used $\alpha_0 = -\infty$ and $\alpha_{t+1} = +\infty$ for notational convenience. We can also eliminate the unobserved variables from the model, and write it directly in terms of the observed variables $\underline{z}_i$. Thus $\underline{z}_i$ is a sequence of discrete random variables, taking values 1,2,...,t+1. We assume

$$\underline{z}_i \text{ independent.} \tag{3a}$$

$$\text{prob}(\underline{z}_i = s) = \Phi((\alpha_s - x_i'\beta)/\sigma) - \Phi((\alpha_{s-1} - x_i'\beta)/\sigma). \tag{3b}$$

Here we have used Φ for the standard normal cumulative distribution function. Also remember that in the discrete normal linear regression model the α_s are given real numbers.

The next generalization is now rather obvious. We assume that the number of steps is still known, but the location of the steps is no longer known. Thus the α_s are t additional parameters, of which it is only known that they are increasing. The resulting *monotone discrete normal linear regression model* is defined by assumptions (4a) and (4b), with (4a) identical to (3a), and with (4b) given by

$$\text{prob}(\underline{z}_i = s) = \Phi(\alpha_s - x_i'\beta) - \Phi(\alpha_{s-1} - x_i'\beta). \tag{4b}$$

In (4b) we have absorbed the parameter σ from (3b) into α and β. The α_s are now unknown, except for their order. Comparing (3b) and (4b) again, we can also say that in the earlier model the α_s are known *up to a linear transformation* (the extra parameter σ), while in the later model the α_s are known *up to a monotone transformation*. If we use terminology from the optimal scaling tradition (De Leeuw, Young, and Takane, 1976, Gifi, 1981, Young, 1981) then the dependent variable is measured on an interval scale for model (3) and on an ordinal scale for model (4).

One further generalization of (4) deserves to be mentioned. In (4) we have used the normal c.d.f. Φ. Models similar to (4), but with other functions in stead of Φ have been proposed by many authors (compare the next section for a partial review). The interesting generalization of (4) assumes that

$$\text{prob}(\underline{z}_i = s) = F(\alpha_s - x_i'\beta) - F(\alpha_{s-1} - x_i'\beta), \tag{5b}$$

with F any c.d.f. This could be called the *monotone discrete nonparametric linear regression model*. We shall make some remarks about possible techniques based on this model in a later section. In the bulk of the paper we concentrate on models (3) and (4), however.

3. SOME HISTORY

The history of the discrete normal linear regression models is very complicated, and our account of it is probably incomplete. We could start the history with Pearson's work on biserial correlation, but this really deals with the situation in which both dependent and independent variables are stochastic. Thus it adresses a somewhat different problem. Perhaps the first appearance of discrete normal linear regression is in *probit analysis*. This was already used by the early psychophysicists Müller and Urban around 1900. The model was called the phi-gamma hypothesis. It only had a single regressor, the physical value of the stimulus. Efficient estimates were computed by weighted linear regression on the transformed proportions, using the 'Müller-Urban weights'. References are in Guilford (1954, chapter 6). Probit analysis is usually attributed to Bliss and Finney, who used the method in bioassay since the thirties. References are in the latest edition of Finney's book on probit analysis (1971). These methods were introduced in econometrics by Tobin (1958), and, in a simultaneous equation context, by Zellner and Lee (1965). Probit models are also popular in the area of modelling discrete choice, although logit models are definitely preferred for choice modelling. An authorative review is given by Manski and McFadden (1981). Probit models were introduced into psychometric test theory by Ferguson and Lawley in the early forties. References are in Lord and Novick (1968, chapter 16, sections on the normal ogive model).

It seems appropriate at this point to point out that probit analysis is a very special case of the discrete normal linear regression model. In the first place the dependent variable in probit analysis is binary: present/absent, dead/alive, correct/wrong, and so on. Extensions to ordered dependent variables with more than two response categories were carried out in biometrics by Aitchison and Silvey (1957), Ashford (1959), Gurland, Lee, and Dahm (1960), and in psychometrics by Samejima (1969). These extensions are all equivalent to our models (3) and (4), although in the biometric literature there is usually only a single regressor and in the psychometric literature this regressor is an unobservable latent trait. There is another, more fundamental sense, in which probit analysis is special. In the classical 'bioassay' problem the independent variable assumes only a small number of values (dosages). For each possible value of x_i there are a large number of replications. In cases such as these it is better to model replications more explicitly. We do this by double indexing. The $\underline{z}_{ij}$ with the same first index, i.e. with the same x_i, are now i.i.d. The $\underline{z}_{ij}$ with a different first index are merely independent. In a particular experiment we have $i=1,\ldots,n$ and $j=1,\ldots,m_i$. We can estimate the probability that $\underline{z}_i = s$ by relative frequencies. And using these probabilities we can apply, for example, the minimum normit chi square method. Or, which is the same thing, weighted least squares with Müller-Urban weights. Thus the probit model, and this is true for the logit and other similar methods as well, is a model which is basically designed for observed proportions. The number of observations is large compared with the number of possible values of the independent variables. There are many replications 'within cells'. The data can be collected in the form of a contingency table with the values of the independent variables defining the rows, and the t+1 possible responses the columns. In the typical social science regression situation we have in mind in this paper the number of values of the independent variables is much too large to make this a practical way of organizing the data. There are too many rows, most cells are empty, the other cells have only a single observation. This makes it impossible to apply minimum normit chi square methods, for example. Maximum likelihood methods (Ashford, 1959, McCullagh, 1980) can still be applied, as we show below. But in probit-like models, and this class includes the discrete choice models of Manski and McFadden and the regression models for ordinal data discussed by McCullagh (1980) and Anderson (1984), the basic statistical reasoning is quite different. In probit models we use asymptotic statistics based on $m_i \to \infty$ for all i. In discrete regression models we use $n \to \infty$. This last form of asymptotic statistics leads to nonstandard results.

It has been pointed out by Amemiya (1973, page 998) that the literature on the estimation of parameters for truncated or censored normal distributions is more closely related to the discrete normal regression problem than the probit literature. Maximum likelihood estimation in truncated normal distributions has been studied in the early fifties by Cohen, Halperin, Hald. This literature is reviewed by Kendall and Stuart (1967, chapter 32). In a biometric context the censored normal distribution was used in survival time research as early as Bliss and Stevens (1937). In the econometric literature the pioneering paper was Tobin (1958). Tobin studied a regression model, which was of the form

$$\underline{z}_i = \max(0, x_i'\beta + \underline{\varepsilon}_i). \tag{6}$$

In fact Tobin considered an apparently more general model, but Amemiya (1973) showed that the additional generality was only apparent. Amemiya also showed that the maximum likelihood estimates behaved properly in Tobin's model, and he provided a convenient consistent initial estimate of the parameters. In Amemiya (1974) the model was extended to multivariate and simultaneous equation models. Rosett and Nelson (1975) extended the Tobin-model to the case in which there are upper limit, lower limit, and non-limit observations. Moreover they made the important extension to the case in which the non-limit values are unknown, which is, in fact, the three-category discrete normal linear regression model. In all papers discussed so far the limit-values (i.e. the α_s of the discrete regression model) are supposed to be known real numbers. The same thing is true in a remarkable biometric paper by Sampford and Taylor (1959), who propose a factorial analysis of variance for censored survival times. The likelihood equations in the paper are solved by a version of the EM-algorithm, that we shall discuss and use more extensively further on.

The monotone discrete normal linear regression model was discussed, in full, for the first time by McKelvey and Zavoina (1975). They define the model, give the likelihood function, differentiate it twice, and discuss a computer program based on Newton's method. Nelson (1976) imbeds the monotone model in a general class of limited dependent variable models, for which he has written a general computer program. Although it may very well be the case that programs based on Newton's method are the most efficient for estimation of parameters, it is also true that the EM-algorithm (Dempster, Laird, Rubin, 1976) provides a lot of insight in the estimation problem and at the same time a very simple algorithm. It has been used for the discrete normal linear regression model, with known bounds, by Wolynetz (1979) and Stewart (1983). A very important theoretical result is that the likelihood function, both for the discrete and for the monotone discrete normal linear regression model, is concave in its parameters. This result was first mentioned by Haberman (in the discussion of McCullagh, 1980), and it was proved, independently it seems, by Burridge (1981) and Pratt (1981). In fact both authors proved it for the more general monotone discrete model given by our (5b), with F not necessary cumulative normal but only restricted to have a strictly log-concave density. Robustness, misspecification, and bias in the Tobit model have recently been investigated by Greene (1981), Nelson (1981), Arabmazar and Schmidt (1982). The book by Manski and McFadden (1981) contains many additional references to closely related work by Lee, Heckman, Hausman, Amemiya, Robinson, Schmidt, and others.

4. ESTIMATION

The technique we use for parameter estimation in this paper is the EM-algorithm, which was introduced in full generality in the statistical literature by Dempster, Laird, and Rubin (1976). In many older papers versions of the EM-algorithm are derived simply by setting the derivatives of the likelihood function equal to zero. The form of the likelihood equations often suggests an iterative algorithm, which is subsequently tried out and found to be convergent. The general theory of the EM-algorithm automatically provides us with a convergence proof, and with information on the speed of convergence (Louis, 1982, Wu, 1983, Boyles, 1983). We shall first adapt the general EM-framework to our discrete regression models.

The function we want to maximize is

$$\underline{L}(\theta) = \sum_{i=1}^{n} \sum_{s=1}^{t+1} \underline{g}_{is} \ln \pi_{is}(\theta), \tag{7}$$

with

$$\pi_{is}(\theta) = \int_{I_s} \phi_i(\theta,x)\,dx. \tag{8}$$

In (7) $\underline{g}_{is}$ indicates what interval observation i is in. Thus $\underline{g}_{is}$ is either zero or one, and for each i only one $\underline{g}_{is}$ is non-zero. I_s in (8) is the interval corresponding with category s, and ϕ_i is the density in cell i, which depends on parameters θ. If $\tilde{\theta}$ is another parameter value, then the Kullback-Leibler inequality (or, if you prefer, the concavity of the logarithm) gives the result

$$\underline{L}(\theta) \geq \underline{L}(\tilde{\theta}) + \{\underline{K}(\theta,\tilde{\theta}) - \underline{K}(\tilde{\theta},\tilde{\theta})\}, \tag{9}$$

with

$$\underline{K}(\theta,\tilde{\theta}) = \sum\sum \underline{g}_{is}\, E_{\tilde{\theta}}(\ln \phi_i(\theta,x) \mid I_s). \tag{10}$$

The M-step of the EM-algorithm maximizes $\underline{K}(\theta,\tilde{\theta})$ over θ, where $\tilde{\theta}$ is the previous value of the parameters. The E-step computes the conditional expectation of the log-density, given that the observation is in I_s, that is required in (10). Observe that if the density is log-concave in the parameters, then $\underline{K}(\theta,\tilde{\theta})$ is concave in θ. Inequality (9) is the key to the convergence proof for the EM-algorithm. If the new estimate of θ is θ^+, then

$$\underline{L}(\theta^+) \geq \underline{L}(\tilde{\theta}) + \{\underline{K}(\theta^+,\tilde{\theta}) - \underline{K}(\tilde{\theta},\tilde{\theta})\} > \underline{L}(\tilde{\theta}) + \{\underline{K}(\tilde{\theta},\tilde{\theta}) - K(\tilde{\theta},\tilde{\theta})\} = \underline{L}(\tilde{\theta}). \tag{11}$$

Thus we increase the likelihood, and if the conditions on the density are sufficient to guarantee that the map $\tilde{\theta} \rightarrow \theta^+$ is continuous, it follows that all accumulation points of the EM-sequence are stationary points of the likelihood function. The concavity result of Haberman, Burridge, and Pratt, mentioned in the previous section, actually shows that the EM-sequence converges to the unique maximum likelihood estimate. The reasoning above assumes that all parameters are under the integration sign, and does not apply directly to the monotone discrete model. It is easy, however, to adapt it to this case by a simple linear change of variables. In our actual computations, however, we solve for the regression parameters for fixed boundaries by EM. We then solve for the boundaries for fixed regression parameters by Newton's method. Alternating these steps gives a convenient convergent algorithm, which is perhaps not optimal in an overall sense, but which has very simple subproblems that fit very conveniently in a matrix-oriented programming language such as APL.

In the case of discrete normal models the conditional expectation in (10) has a simple explicit form. It was already derived in this context by Wolynetz (1979) and Stewart (1983). First define $\tilde{w}_{is} = (\alpha_s - x_i'\tilde{\beta})/\tilde{\sigma}$. Also

$$\tilde{\kappa}_{is} = (\phi(\tilde{w}_{is}) - \phi(\tilde{w}_{i,s-1}))/(\Phi(\tilde{w}_{is}) - \Phi(\tilde{w}_{i,s-1})), \tag{12}$$

$$\tilde{\tau}_{is} = 1 - (\tilde{w}_{is}\phi(\tilde{w}_{is}) - \tilde{w}_{i,s-1}\phi(\tilde{w}_{i,s-1}))/(\Phi(\tilde{w}_{is}) - \Phi(\tilde{w}_{i,s-1})), \tag{13}$$

$$\tilde{y}_{is} = x_i'\tilde{\beta} - \tilde{\sigma}\tilde{\kappa}_{is}. \tag{14}$$

Then

$$\underline{K}(\theta,\tilde{\theta}) = -\tfrac{1}{2}\{n \ln \sigma^2 + \sigma^{-2}(\tilde{\sigma}^2 \sum\sum_{is} \underline{g}_{is}(\tilde{\tau}_{is} - \tilde{\kappa}^2_{is}) + \sum_i (x_i'\beta - \sum_s \underline{g}_{is}\tilde{y}_{is})^2\}. \tag{15}$$

It is immediately clear from (14) that

$$\beta^+ = (X'X)^{-1}X'\tilde{y} = \tilde{\beta} - \tilde{\sigma}(X'X)^{-1}X'\tilde{\kappa}. \tag{16}$$

Moreover, using some obvious additional notation,

$$(\sigma^2)^+ = n^{-1}\{\tilde{\sigma}^2 \sum_i \tilde{\upsilon}_i + \sum_i (x_i'\beta^+ - \tilde{y}_i)^2\}. \tag{17}$$

This is different from the update-formula of Wolynetz and Stewart, who have

$$(\sigma^2)^+ = \sum_i (x_i'\beta^+ - \tilde{y}_i)^2 / \sum_i (1 - \tilde{\upsilon}_i). \tag{18}$$

Although (18), if convergent, leads to the maximum likelihood solution, it does not seem to follow directly from the usual EM-steps.

The algorithm described by (16) and (17) is exceedingly simple to carry out. It consists of a sequence of simple OLS regressions, which are guaranteed to converge to the maximum likelihood solution. Convergence may be slow, but because the iterations are very simple it does not matter if we have to perform a lot of them. Numerical comparions with the Newton-Raphson method are in Burridge (1981).

5. BIAS IN OLS ESTIMATES

Suppose the discrete regression model is misspecified as a continuous model, and parameters are estimated by ordinary least squares. Then clearly the resulting estimates will not be consistent. To study inconsistency in this context we assume, following Greene (1981) and Stewart (1983), the slightly different model

$$\underline{y}_i = \mu + \underline{x}_i'\beta + \underline{\varepsilon}_i, \tag{19a}$$

$$(\underline{x}_i, \underline{\varepsilon}_i) \text{ i.i.d.} \tag{19b}$$

Model (2) differs from (19) in two important respects. In the first place the disturbances in (2) are assumed to be normally distributed, and in the second place the regressors in (2) are fixed. In (19) we assume random regressors, and no normality. We do assume, in addition,

$$E(\underline{\varepsilon}_i) = 0 \text{ and } E(\underline{\varepsilon}_i \underline{x}_i') = 0 \text{ for all } i. \tag{19c}$$

And, of course,

$$\underline{z}_i = \phi(\underline{y}_i), \text{ with } \phi \text{ a monotone step function.} \tag{19d}$$

Model (2) and model (19) are different, although it will be impossible to distinguish them on the basis of empirical data alone. We shall study bias and inconsistency of OLS estimation in model (19), assuming that the results are of relevance also to model (2). This somewhat devious path is followed because model (19) is much simpler, and because 'usually' results derived for 'structural' models such as (19) are also relevant for their 'functional' versions such as (2).

The OLS estimates of β in model (19) are of the form

$$\hat{\beta} = S_{XX}^{-1} S_{XG} \eta, \tag{20}$$

where S_{XX} is the observed covariance matrix of the regressors, where S_{XG} is the observed covariance between the regressors and the column of the indicator matrix $\underline{G}$ with elements $\underline{g}_{is}$, and where η contains scores for the categories. Column s of S_{XG} converges in probability to $\pi_s(E_s(\underline{x}) - m_x)$, where $E_s(\underline{x})$ is the conditional expectation of $\underline{x}$ if $\underline{y}$ is in I_s, where π_s is the content of I_s, and m_x the expected value of x. Now assume that *the regression of $\underline{x}$ on $\underline{y}$ is linear*. Then column s of S_{XG} converges to $\xi_s \Sigma\beta$, where $\Sigma = \text{plim } S_{XX}$ and $\xi_s = \pi_s(\bar{y}_s - \bar{y})/\sigma_y^2$. Here $\bar{y}_s$ is the conditional expectation of y, given that it is in interval I_s. Observe that the ξ_s sum to zero. It follows that $\text{plim } S_{XX}^{-1} S_{XG} = \beta\xi'$, and thus $\text{plim } \hat{\beta} = (\xi'\eta)\beta$. This generalizes results of Stewart (1983), who assumes that the regressors are normally distributed. Our results can be used to derive simple consistent estimates of β by using the fact that $S_{XX}^{-1}S_{XG}$ converges to a rank-one matrix. We can also use the results on optimal quantization, reviewed in Gifi (1981, section 12.3.3), to bound the bias $\xi'\eta$, and to show that the bias disappears if we let $t \to \infty$ (and choose the scores in appropriate ways). Detailed results will be published at another occasion.

OLS-bias can also be studied in a somewhat different way, following Don (1981) and Dempster and Rubin (1983). We write the likelihood equation for β_j in the form, using $\underline{z}$ for a standard normal variable,

$$\sum\sum \underline{g}_{is} E\{\underline{z} \mid (\alpha_{s-1} - x_i'\beta)/\sigma < \underline{z} < (\alpha_s - x_i'\beta)/\sigma\} x_{ij} = 0. \tag{21}$$

Now let $\eta_s = \frac{1}{2}(\alpha_s + \alpha_{s-1})$ and let $\delta_s = \alpha_s - \alpha_{s-1}$. If δ_s is small compared to σ, then the conditional expectation in (21) can be replaced by its Sheppard-approximation. If we substitute this in (21) we obtain

$$\sum (1 - \underline{\delta}_i^2/12\sigma^2)(\underline{\eta}_i - x_i'\beta)x_{ij} = 0, \tag{22}$$

where $\underline{\eta}_i$ is the midpoint and $\underline{\delta}_i$ the length of the interval that observation i is in. If we solve (22) for β we have applied a form of Sheppard's correction or a correction for continuity. A similar development is possible if we want to estimate the variance parameter σ. We write the likelihood equation in the form

$$\sum\sum \underline{g}_{is} E\{\underline{z}^2 \mid (\alpha_{s-1} - x_i'\beta)/\sigma < \underline{z} < (\alpha_s - x_i'\beta)/\sigma\} = n. \tag{23}$$

If we substitute the approximation of the conditional expectation, then this becomes

$$\frac{1}{12}\sum \underline{\delta}_i^2 + \sum (1 - \frac{1}{6}\underline{\delta}_i^2/\sigma^2)(\underline{\eta}_i - x_i'\beta)^2 = n\sigma^2. \tag{24}$$

If we want to solve (22) and (24) we have to decide what to do which the two extreme categories first, because δ_s and η_s are not defined for those categories. If all δ_s are equal, excepting the end-categories of course, then (22) shows that the approximate maximum likelihood estimates are the least squares estimates using the midpoints. This is different from Don (1981) and Dempster and Rubin (1983), but they work with model (19) in which also the regressors are random or are rounded.

We briefly summarize our results on bias. If the intervals are small compared with the variance of the disturbances, then (22) and (24) show that OLS on the midpoints will not be far off. These equations also show how OLS estimates can be corrected, but we do not know if these corrections are really useful. In the examples we have analyzed, which are reported below, the approximation conditions are clearly not met. In model (19), which can be used as another type of approximation to model (2), we have seen that OLS is consistent 'up to a scale factor' provided the regression of the predictors on the criterion is linear. For completeness we also mention a result of Ruud (1983), who analyzes (19) completed with distributional assumptions for $\underline{x}_i$ and $\underline{\varepsilon}_i$. Ruud proves, that if the regression of the components of $\underline{x}_i$ on $\underline{y}_i$ is linear, then the maximum likelihood estimates of β are consistent 'up to a scale factor' even if the distribution of $\underline{\varepsilon}_i$ is incorrectly specified. Sampford and Taylor (1959) point out, correctly, that the maximum likelihood estimate of the variance parameter is biased and inconsistent in the continuous regression model. In the discrete models this bias persists, and they discuss several correction methods. Of course the bias is most serious if the number of parameters is large compared with the number of observations. This will be the case in analysis of variance and analysis of covariance type situations, with a single observation in each cell. In the more usual regression situations the bias will be quite small.

6. RELATIONSHIPS WITH OPTIMAL SCALING

We have already shown that the EM algorithm for discrete normal linear regression models amounts to performing a sequence of ordinary linear regressions on data transformed by using the E-step. The transformations are given explicitly by equation (14). This particular algorithm is useful because it shows in what way maximum likelihood estimation is connected with optimal scaling and partial least squares theory.

In the optimal scaling approach to discrete linear regression or monotone linear regression (Kruskal, 1965, De Leeuw, Young, and Takane, 1976, Young, De Leeuw, Takane, 1976, Gifi, 1981) two types of projection algorithms are alternated iteratively. In the first projection the currently optimally scaled data are projected on the subspace defined by the regression model. This is OLS estimation of the regression parameters. In the second projection the predicted or expected values are projected on the cone of feasible quantifications, which gives new optimal quantifications for the current regression estimates. And so on. The technique is not derived from a particular probability model. It simply starts from the fact that the predicted values are in a given subspace (spanned by the regressors). The feasible quantifications (which must be monotone with the data) are in a convex cone. We are looking for two vectors, one in the cone and one in the subspace, with an angle between them that is as small as possible. Different 'measurement levels' define different cones of feasible quantifications, but the basic idea is the purely geometrical one outlined above.

The optimal scaling approach, which has been extended to many nonlinear models by Gifi (1981), is quite similar to the PLS-approach of Wold. The PLS approach is explained in Jöreskog and Wold (1982). The basic idea is that a simultaneous equation system is constructed using latent variables. Each latent variable has various observed indicators associated with it. The PLS method consists of two steps: in the first step a 'proxy' is computed for each latent variable by making suitable linear combinations of the indicators, and in the second step these currently optimal estimates of the latent variables are used to fit the (recursive) simultaneous equations. Again these two steps are alternated iteratively, until convergence is obtained.

Thus we can say that optimal scaling and PLS define their models in terms of unobserved variables. In optimal scaling the quantification is unknown, or only partially known. In PLS the latent variables are unobserved, but partially known through their indicators. It is clear that the EM-algorithm for discrete regression can be interpreted in exactly the same way as the alternating least squares methods for optimal scaling. The 'optimal' transformation (for current best regression estimates) is now given by the E-step. It is not dictated by purely geometrical considerations any more, but it is influenced strongly by the choice of the probability model. As a consequence it is, in a well defined sense, optimal for the given model, and suboptimal for other models. The optimal scaling transformation (which is often 'monotone regression') may not be optimal in the statistical sense for any particular model, although it is of course optimal in the geometrical sense. According to PLS-adepts the estimates they compute have two major advantages over maximum likelihood estimates for the simultaneous equation system with latent variables. The first advantage is that PLS also estimates the latent variables, and not only the structural parameters of the covariance matrix. It follows directly from the general theory of the EM-algorithm that this is merely a question of algorithm choice. We can compute maximum likelihood estimates by using the EM-method, which computes 'proxies' for the latent variables in the E-step. It can be argued that the EM-proxies are even better than the PLS-proxies, because using EM-proxies leads to consistent estimation of the structural parameters, while using PLS-proxies does not (Dijkstra, 1983). The second acclaimed advantage of PLS is that it may not be optimal in terms of statistical efficiency, but it is optimal in terms of prediction efficiency. This is a very complicated claim, whose precise meaning is not clear to me, but it may be possible to translate this claim in terms of robustness or in terms of the geometry of least squares.

Be this as it may, purely computational considerations suggest that the optimal data transformations from the E-step of the EM-algorithm may have advantages over the cone-projection steps of optimal scaling algorithms as well. Cone projection works on the outside of the cone, and large cones contain many possibilities for 'degenerate' solutions. It seems that, even in nonlinear cases such as multidimensional scaling or principal component analysis, the EM-transformation is less susceptible to degeneracy. Moreover it is statistically optimal in at least one well-defined model, which may be interesting in cases in which we are fairly confident that this model makes sense.

7. SOME EXAMPLES

The model example we use is the serological readings example from Fisher's 'Statistical methods for research workers'. In the 1970 edition it is example 46.2, and it occurs on page 291-300. 'Twelve samples of human blood tested with twelve different sera gave reactions represented by the five symbols -, ?, w, (+), and +.' (l.c., pag 291). Thus the data are a 12 x 12 ANOVA table, with one qualitative observation in each cell. The categories are supposed to be ordered, but this is all we know. Fisher analyzes the data by, essentially, correspondence analysis. We shall analyze them by using our regression methods.

For the analysis we have used a provisory computerprogram MONREG, written in APL. It fits both the discrete and the monotone normal linear regression model by using the Newton-Raphson method to maximize the (concave) log-likelihood function. We do not present the results in detail, but we outline some of the tentative conclusions from the analysis. The log-likelihood for the OLS-solution, using scores 1-5 for the categories, is -74.2155. The discrete linear normal model, with the data intervals equally spaced, category s being interpreted as between $s - \frac{1}{2}$ and $s + \frac{1}{2}$, has a maximum log-likelihood of -68.4316. The estimates of the regression parameters are very close to the OLS estimates, the residual variance is about 2/3 of the OLS residual variance. If we assume that the ML estimates for the discrete linear model are the true values, then we can compute bias and dispersion of OLS estimates. The bias is small, and the dispersion of the OLS estimates is smaller than that of the ML estimates. In fact the mean square error of the OLS estimates is less than the approximate mean square error of the ML estimates. Thus the biased OLS estimates outperform the ML estimates in this respect. The maximum log-likelihood for the monotone model is -57.4829. The estimates of the regression parameters are not very well behaved in this model. The maximum is along a direction of recession of the likelihood function, which some parameters tending to infinity. The information matrix is singular at the maximum likelihood estimate, which causes the Newton method to converge only linearly, and which gives estimates of the sampling variances which are difficult to interpret.

Of course the Fisher example is somewhat special, because the number of regression parameters is large compared to the number of observations. We have also analyzed other examples, varying from ordinary bivariate linear regression to covariance analysis. The Newton algorithm is usually well behaved, and even if some parameters tend to infinity the maximum of the likelihood is still well defined. It is clear from our examples that the concavity of the log-likelihood is a very important property. In many cases it would be difficult to recognize convergence or to know when to stop if concavity would not obtain.

Many things must still be investigated. The results on OLS bias in section 5 have not been investigated for practical usefulness. The precise condition under which parameter estimates tend to infinity have not been established. The nature of the 'optimal' transformation found by the ML-methods has not been studied in any detail. The conditions under which MSE of OLS is less than MSE of ML could also be made more precise, perhaps. All these loose ends call for further investigation. It is of course very important to find out if and in how far our results can be generalized to nonlinear models such as principal component analysis and multidimensional scaling. Optimal scaling methods of the alternating least squares type have been extended to many nonlinear models (Gifi, 1981), and we can perhaps hope that the discrete ML methods generalize equally easily.

8. SOME GENERALIZATIONS

We have already mentioned generalization to nonlinear models in the previous section. This is straightforward, and theoretically not exceptionally interesting. Generalizations such as these are mainly of an algorithmic nature. In this section we point out two types of generalizations which are of a more theoretical nature. They also have major consequences for the algorithms, but these consequences tend to go somewhat deeper.

To discuss the first generalization we remember that the regressors are mapped linearly into the real line, by using a weighted combination. The real line is partioned into intervals, and the probabilities of the responses are integrals over the intervals. These intervals correspond with parallel strips in the regressor space. The generalization is to map the regressors into higher dimensional space, by making more than one linear combination, and to define response probabilities by integrating over non-parallel regions that partition this space. We can think of quadrants, or rectangles, for instance. This is the natural multidimensional generalization of the discrete regression models we have studied. It is consequently not at all true that the grouped continuous approach is limited to one-dimensional models, as Anderson (1984) maintains.

The second generalization steers away from the cumulative normal in (3b) or (4b), using a general F as in (5b). Thus we do not substitute another fixed cdf, such as the logistic or double exponential (discussed extensively by McCullagh,, 1980), but we leave F free. It follows form the properties of general moment problems (a recent review is given in the book by Krein and Nudelman, 1977) that we can suppose without loss of generality that F is a step function. Alternatively we can approximate F by using splines. It is useful to use integrated B-splines for this purpose, because they have the properties of distribution functions, and because B-splines are log-concave on the interval in which they are positive. And log-concavity of the density guarantees concavity of the log-likelihood, according to the result of Burridge and Pratt we discussed earlier. The log-concavity of B-splines is proved in the basic paper by Curry and Schoenberg (1966, theorem 3). Integrated B-splines have been used in data analysis for a rather similar purpose by Winsberg and Ramsay (1981).

It is clear that our suggested generalizations are tentative. The results of our simpler program, with linear models and a completely determined univariate cdf, will indicate if the thought of generalization is at all useful. If the monotone normal linear regression model already has too many parameters to be well-conditioned, then obviously in such cases further generalization would be useless. Much additional work with simpler models is needed, before these generalizations can be attempted. Perhaps most urgently we need to study the speed of convergence of the maximum likelihood estimates to their theoretical limit distributions. If this is already very slow in the simpler models, then the theoretical consistency and efficiency of ML are not very important from a practical point of view. In this case there is room for theoretically less satisfactory, but practically perhaps preferable alternatives. It could very well be that OLS estimation is one such useful alternative.

9. REFERENCES

Aitchison, J. and Silvey, S.D. The generalization of probit analysis to the case of multiple responses. Biometrika, 1957, 44, 131-140.

Amemiya, T. Regression analysis when the dependent variable is truncated normal. Econometrica, 1973, 41, 997-1016.

Amemiya, T. Multivariate regression and simultaneous equation models when the dependent variables are truncated normal. Econometrica, 1974, 42, 999-1012.

Anderson, J.A. Regression and ordered categorical variables. Journal of the Royal Statitiscal Society(B), 1984, 46, 1-30.

Arabmazar, A. and Schmidt, P. An investigation of the robustness of the Tobit estimator to non-normality. Econometrica, 1982, 50, 1055-1063.

Ashford, J.R. An approach to the analysis of data for semi-quantal responses in biological assay. Biometrics, 1959, 15, 573-581.

Bliss, C.I. and Stevens, W.L. The calculation of the time-mortality curve. Annals of Applied Biology, 1937, 24, 815-852.

Boyles, R.A. On the convergence of the EM algorithm. Journal of the Royal Statistical Society, 1983, 45, 47-50.

Burridge, J. A note on maximum likelihood estimation for regression models using grouped data. Journal of the Royal Statistical Society(B), 1981, 43, 41-45.

Curry, H.B. and Schoenberg, I.J. On Polya frequency functions IV: The fundamental spline functions and their limits. Journal d'Analyse Mathematique, 1966, 17, 71-107.

De Leeuw, J. Models and methods for the analysis of correlation coefficients. Journal of Econometrics, 1983, 22, 113-138.

De Leeuw, J., Young, F.W., & Takane, Y. Additive structure in qualitative data: an alternating least squares method with optimal scaling features. Psychometrika, 1976, 41, 471-503.

Dempster, A.P., Laird, N.M., & Rubin, D.B. Maximum likelihood from incomplete data using the EM algorithm. Journal of the Royal Statistical Society(B), 1977, 39, 1-38.

Dempster, A.P. and Rubin, D.B. Rounding error in regression: the appropriateness of Sheppard's corrections. Journal of the Royal Statistical Society(B), 1983, 45, 51-59.

Don, F.J.H. A note on Sheppard's corrections for grouping and maximum likelihood estimation. Journal of Multivariate Analysis, 1981, 11, 452-458.

Dijkstra, T. Some comments on maximum likelihood and partial least squares. Journal of Econometrics, 1983, 22, 67-90.

Fienberg, S.E. The analysis of cross-classified data. Cambridge (Ma), MIT-Press, 1980.

Finney, D. Probit analysis. Cambridge, Cambridge University Press, 1971.

Fisher, R.A. Statististical methods for research workers. (14e edition). Edinburgh, Oliver and Boyd, 1970.

Gifi, A. Nonlinear multivariate analysis. Leiden, Department of Data Theory, 1981.

Greene, W.H. On the asymptotic bias of the ordinary least squares estimator in the Tobit model. Econometrica, 1981, 49, 505-513.

Guilford, J.P. Psychometric methods. (2e edition). New York, McGraw-Hill, 1954.

Gurland, J., Lee, I., & Dahm, P.A. Polychotomous quantal response in biological assay. Biometrics, 1960, 16, 382-398.

Hemelrijk, J. Underlining random variables. Statistica Neerlandica, 1966, 20, 1-8.

Jöreskog, K.G. and Wold, H.O.A. Systems under indirect observation. Amsterdam, North Holland Publishing Company, 1982.

Kendall, M.G. and Stuart, A. The advanced theory of statistics. Volume II, 2e edition, London, Griffin, 1967.

Krein, M.G. and Nudelman, A.A. The Markov moment problem and extrremal problems. Providence (RI), American Mathematical Society, 1977.

Kruskal, J.B. Analysis of factorial experiments by estimating monotone transformations of the data. Journal of the Royal Statistical Society, 1965, 27, 251-263.

Lord, F.M. and Novick, M.R. Statistical theories of mental test scores. Reading (Ma), Addison-Wesley, 1967.

Louis, T.A. Finding the observed information matrix when using the EM Algorithm. Journal of the Royal Statistical Society(B), 1982, 44, 226-233.

McCullagh, P. Regression models for ordinal data. Journal of the Royal Statistical Society, 1980, 42, 109-142.

McKelvey, R.D. and Zavoina, W. A statistical model for the analysis of ordinal level dependent variables. Journal of Mathematical Sociology, 1975, 4, 103-120.

Manski, C.F. and McFadden, D. Structural analysis of discrete data with econometric applications. Cambridge (Ma), MIT Press, 1981.

Nelson, F.D. On a general computer algorithm for the analysis of models with limited dependent variables. Annals of economic and social measurement, 1976, 5, 493-509.

Nelson, F.D. A test for misspecification in the censored normal model. Econometrica, 1981, 49, 1317-1329.

Pratt, J.W. Concavity of the log likelihood. Journal of the American Statistical Association, 1981, 76, 103-106.

Rosett, R.N. and Nelson, F.D. Estimation of the two-limit probit regression model. Econometrica, 1975, 43, 141-146.

Samejima, F. Estimation of latent ability using a response pattern of graded scores. Psychometric Monograph, no 17, 1969.

Sampford, M.R. and Taylor, J. Censored observations in randomized block experiments. Journal of the Royal Statistical Society, 1959, 21, 214-237.

Stewart, M.B. On least squares estimation when the dependent variable is grouped. Review of economic studies, 1983, 50, 737-753.

Tobin, J. Estimation of relationships for limited dependent variables. Econometrica, 1958, 26, 24-36.

Winsberg, S. and Ramsay, J.O. Analysis of pairwise preference data using integrated B-splines. Psychometrika, 1981, 46, 171-186.

Winship, C. and Mare, R.D. Structural equations and path analysis for discrete data. American Journal of Sociology, 1983, 89, 54-110.

Wolynetz, M.C. Maximum likelihood estimation in a linear model from confined and censored data. Applied Statistics, 1979, 28, 196-206.

Wu, C.F.J. On the convergence properties of the EM algorithm. The Annals of Statistics, 1983, 11, 95-103.

Young, F.W., De Leeuw, J., & Takane, Y. Regression with qualitative and quantitative variables: an alternating least squares method with optimal scaling features. Psychometrika, 1976, 40, 505-529.

Zellner, A. and Lee, T.H. Joint eestimation of relationships involving discrete random variables. Econometrica, 1965, 33, 382-394.

Ruud, P.A. Sufficient conditions for the consistency of maximum likelihood estimates despite misspecification of distribution in multinomial discrete choice models. Econometrica, 1983, 51, 225-228.

Added in proof

Both Theo Dijkstra and Tom Wansbeek have pointed out to me that the results of Green, Stewart, and Ruud, which were generalized in section 5, have also been generalized, in a very similar way, by Chung and Goldberger (Proportional projections in limited dependent variable models, Econometrica, 1984, 52, 531-534).

SPECIFICATION IN SIMULTANEOUS LINEAR EQUATIONS MODELS: THE RELATION BETWEEN A PRIORI SPECIFICATIONS AND RESULTING ESTIMATORS

Bernard M.S. van Praag
Econometric Institute
Erasmus University Rotterdam
Burgemeester Oudlaan 50
3062 PA ROTTERDAM, The Netherlands

Jan T.A. Koster
Sociological Institute of Leyden University
Stationsplein 242
2312 AR LEYDEN, The Netherlands

0. ABSTRACT

The estimation of coefficients of a linear model is discussed, where we do not assume that the random vector X satisfies the model, but that the model is only a model of best fit. We consider both the situation without additional constraints on the coefficients and the situation with differentiable constraints. In both cases, the vector of parameters is a differentiable function of a covariance matrix, making the δ-method applicable. It is shown that the asymptotic distribution of the estimators is normal. Closed formulas for their asymptotic covariance matrices are derived.

1. INTRODUCTION

Let X, a random (row-)vector taking values in R^k, be a phenomenon that we like to describe by means of a rough descriptive model. We suspect approximate relationships between the components of X of the type f(x) = 0. The equation or set of equations f(x) = 0 is called the model that approximately describes those presumed relationships. We do not pretend that nature behaves accordingly, but only that the model

----

*The paper has been written when the first author was at the Center for Research in Public Economics and was a fellow at the Netherlands Institute for the Advanced Study in the Humanities and Social Sciences (N.I.A.S.) at Wassenaar. We are grateful for the valuable support of Bertram Wesselman, research fellow of the Netherlands Organization for the Advancement of Pure Research (Z.W.O.).

furnishes an acceptable shorthand description of the phenomenon X we consider. In general we consider parameterized models of the type $f(x,B) = 0$. In this paper we restrict ourselves still further to the linear type, that is

$$f(x,B) = xB = 0 \tag{1.1}$$

where B is an unknown parameter matrix of order $k \times p$ that has to be estimated. We call (1.1) a linear model.

One of the strategies to handle this kind of problems is to introduce an observation error ε and write $X = \xi + \varepsilon$. Then it is assumed that ε is $N(0,\Sigma)$-distributed and that the model (1.1) holds exactly for the 'true' values ξ. The vector ξ is taken to be either non-random, in which case we have the functional model or multivariate normal with $E\xi = 0$; the latter case is called the structural model (see e.g. Keller and Wansbeek (1983)). In both cases we have $XB = \varepsilon B = \eta$ (say) and the distribution of η has a specific form. Its density element can be written down, and by means of that we may calculate the density of a random sample $X_1,\ldots,X_T$ and maximize the sample density with respect to B. Traditional ML-theory provides us with the estimator $\hat{B}$ and an estimate of its precision in terms of its covariance matrix.

The weakness of such an approach is, in our opinion, that the result is dependent on the validity of the a priori assumptions concerning the distribution of X of which we do not know too much. If we do not assume any knowledge of the distribution of X (except for the existence of certain moments of X) then the ML-approach cannot be applied. It is therefore that we want to develop an assumption-free (or distribution free) approach, much in the spirit of Pearson (1901) and Huber (1981). Similar results but in a different context have been derived by White (1980,1982).

Van Praag (1983) considers the question how B in (1.1) is estimated and gives the probability distribution of the estimator $\hat{B}$ in large samples.

In this paper we generalize the problem by posing additional differentiable constraints on B, say $h(B) = 0$, analogous to the way in which Aitchison and Silvey (1958), Silvey (1959), and Lee and Bentler (1980) provide generalizations of the ML-method by adding differentiable constraints.

Suppose $S = \{x \mid f(x) = 0\}$ is a proper subset of R^k. Let $||.||$ denote the Euclidean norm on R^k. In order to check whether a specific observation x fits the model, it is natural to consider the distance between x and S, defined as $d(x,S) = \inf_{y \in S} ||x - y||$. If this distance is small, x satisfies the model more or less, otherwise not. In the same way the average fit of the model can be evaluated by $E(d(X,S))$. If S is described by $f(x,B) = 0$ where B is a parameter matrix, the average distance of x to S depends on B as well. The best fitting S is then found by minimizing $Ed(x,S(B))$ with respect to B.

The usual situation in econometric and sociometric modelling is that some coefficients (effects) are set at zero or are required to equal others. These constraints, described by $h(B) = 0$, may arise from theoretical knowledge about the relations between the effects, or simply from identification requirements without serious theoretical underpinning. In the latter case the constraints have an *ad hoc* character.

In this paper the function h does not need to be linear; the only requirement is that it is twice differentiable.

The paper is structured as follows. In Section 2 some notations are introduced and the population-sample decomposition (PSD) principle, based on the so-called δ-method, is described. In Section 3 the objective function is derived and the solution for the unconstrained case is given. In Section 4 the case with *a priori* constraints of the form $h(B) = 0$ is studied. Section 5 concludes. Finally, in Appendix 2, explicit expressions for the results concerning the covariance matrices from Section 4 are derived; some matrix notations for derivatives are given in Appendix 1.

2. PRELIMINARIES AND NOTATIONS

In the following sections elements of R^m will be written as *row* vectors (for each $m \in N$). $||.||_Q$ will denote the norm on R^m defined by $||x||_Q^2 = xQx'$, where the prime denotes (matrix) transposition and Q is assumed to be positive-definite. If $Q = I$ we will simply write $||.||$ instead of $||.||_I$.

Let A be a m×n matrix. By $\tilde{A} \in R^{mn}$ we will denote $\tilde{A} = (\text{vec } A)' = (a_{11}, a_{21}, \ldots, a_{m1}, a_{12}, \ldots, a_{mn})$. The same notation is used for matrix-valued functions f, that is, $\tilde{f} = (\text{vec } f)'$. If the matrix A is of full rank n, P(A) will denote the matrix $A(A'A)^{-1}A'$ of order m×m. It is easy to see that P(A) is the orthogonal projection of R^m on the space spanned by the columns of A.

In this and the next section X is a random vector taking values in R^k.

The covariance matrix of X, assumed to be non-singular, will be denoted by Σ. Since we will assume that $EX = 0$, we have $\Sigma = EX'X$. Writing $X = (x_1,..,x_k)$, the typical element of Σ is Ex_ix_j, which we denote by σ_{ij}. The p eigenvectors of Σ associated with the p smallest eigenvalues will be called the p minimal eigenvectors of Σ. It is furthermore assumed that X has finite fourth-order moments $Ex_ix_jx_kx_\ell$, denoted by $m_{ijk\ell}$.

We are interested in the estimation of population parameters that are themselves differentiable functions of the second order population moments; we call them covariance functions. These functions are studied in multivariate analysis (e.g. regression analysis, principal components). As the sample moments of a random sample are consistent estimators of the population moments, consistent estimators of the values of the covariance functions may be obtained by replacing the population covariance matrix Σ by its sample analogue $\hat{\Sigma}_T$. For instance, if f is a continuous function, a consistent estimator of $f(\Sigma)$ is $f(\hat{\Sigma}_T)$, where $\hat{\Sigma}_T$ is the sample covariance matrix.

In order to derive the large-sample distribution of the estimator $f(\hat{\Sigma}_T)$ we use a theorem that may be proved by means of the δ-method (cf. Cramér (1946), Rao (1973)).

Theorem: Let $\hat{\theta}_T$ be a k-dimensional random vector and let θ be a k-dimensional vector parameter. Assume that $\hat{\theta}_T$ has an asymptotic normal distribution, that is

$$\sqrt{T}\,(\hat{\theta}_T - \theta) \overset{L}{\to} N(0,V(\theta)) .$$

Let f be a function defined on an open neighbourhood of θ, taking values in R^m and assume that f is differentiable at θ. Then $\sqrt{T}\,(f(\hat{\theta}_T) - f(\theta)) \overset{L}{\to} N(0, (\frac{df}{d\theta})V(\theta)(\frac{df}{d\theta})')$, where $\frac{df}{d\theta}$ stands for the gradient vector or matrix of f.

Now suppose a sequence of random k-vectors $X_1,X_2,..,X_T,...$ that are independent and have the same distribution as X. Then by the Lindeberg-Levy Central Limit Theorem $\sqrt{T}\,(\tilde{\hat{\Sigma}}_T - \tilde{\Sigma}) \overset{L}{\to} N(0,V)$, where

$\hat{\Sigma}_T = \frac{1}{T} \sum_{t=1}^{T} X_t'X_t$ is the sample covariance matrix with elements

$\hat{\sigma}_{ij} = \frac{1}{T} \sum_{t=1}^{T} x_{it}x_{jt}$, and V denotes the covariance matrix of the random

matrix $X'X$, so a typical element of V is $\text{cov}(x_ix_j, x_kx_\ell) = m_{ijk\ell} - \sigma_{ij}\sigma_{k\ell}$

(see e.g. Muirhead (1982)).
If f is a differentiable covariance function, then $\sqrt{T}\,(f(\hat{\Sigma}_T) - f(\Sigma))$ is asymptotically normal with mean zero, and covariance matrix

$$(\frac{df}{d\underset{\sim}{\Sigma}}(\Sigma))V(\frac{df}{d\underset{\sim}{\Sigma}}(\Sigma))'. \tag{2.1}$$

This asymptotic covariance matrix may be estimated consistently by

$$(\frac{df}{d\underset{\sim}{\Sigma}}(\hat{\Sigma}_T))\hat{V}(\frac{df}{d\underset{\sim}{\Sigma}}(\hat{\Sigma}_T))', \tag{2.2}$$

where $\hat{V}$ is a consistent estimator of V with typical element

$$\hat{m}_{ijk\ell} - \hat{\sigma}_{ij}\hat{\sigma}_{k\ell}, \text{ where } \hat{m}_{ijk\ell} = \frac{1}{T}\sum_{t=1}^{T} x_{it}x_{jt}x_{kt}x_{\ell t}. \tag{2.3}$$

Note that in (2.2) we can distinguish a <u>population</u> part (namely $\frac{df}{d\underset{\sim}{\Sigma}}$) and a <u>sample</u> part $\hat{V}$. It is therefore that we speak about the <u>population-sample decomposition</u> (cf. Van Praag (1983)). The usefulness of this distinction derives from the fact that results concerning the population part $\frac{df}{d\underset{\sim}{\Sigma}}$ remain valid notwithstanding possible sample problems like incomplete observations, selectivity bias etc. In these cases $\sqrt{T}\,(f(\hat{\Sigma}_T) - f(\Sigma))$ remains asymptotically normal with mean zero and covariance matrix (2.1), as long as the estimator $\hat{\Sigma}_T$ is itself an asymptotically normal consistent estimator of Σ. The only change is then that the covariance matrix V has to be assessed by an <u>ad hoc</u> method instead of applying (2.3). For a specific example of this approach we refer to Van Praag, Dijkstra and Van Velzen (1984).

3. <u>THE UNCONSTRAINED CASE</u>

Suppose B is a matrix of order k×p. Denote by G(B) the collection of all mappings from R^k to the subspace $\{x \in R^k \mid xB = 0\}$ that are Borel-measurable. An element of G(B) will be denoted by g_B. The problem is to find a matrix B_0 (of fixed order k×p) and a mapping $g_0 \in G(B_0)$ such that

$$E\,||X - g_0(X)||_Q^2 = \min E\,||X - g_B(X)||_Q^2, \tag{3.1}$$

where the minimum is taken over all matrices B of order k×p, and all $g_B \in G(B)$. It is well-known that - for a fixed matrix B and for all $x \in R^k$ - the minimum of $||x - g_B(x)||_Q^2$ is assumed when $g_B(x)$ =

$x(I - B(B'Q^{-1}B)^{-1}B'Q^{-1})$. So the righthand side of (3.1) equals

$$\min E \; || XB(B'Q^{-1}B)^{-1}B'Q^{-1} ||^2_Q , \tag{3.2}$$

(see Pollock (1979)) where the minimum is taken over all matrices B of order k×p. Now, since

$$E \; || XB(B'QB)^{-1}B'Q^{-1} ||^2_Q = E \; XB(B'Q^{-1}B)^{-1}B'X'$$
$$= \operatorname{tr} B(B'Q^{-1}B)^{-1}B'\Sigma , \tag{3.3}$$

the minimization problem (3.2) boils down to finding a matrix B for which $\operatorname{tr} B(B'Q^{-1}B)^{-1}B'\Sigma$ is minimal. We call this the <u>unconstrained</u> minimization problem since there are no restrictions on the matrix B (except for its order). The <u>constrained</u> problem is then easy to formulate, viz., we require the solution of (3.2) under differentiable side-conditions $h(B) = \underset{\sim}{0}$. These problems are <u>population</u> problems as only the gradient matrix $\frac{d\underset{\sim}{B}}{d\Sigma}(\Sigma)$ is needed. If $Q = I$, the r.h.s. of (3.3) equals $\operatorname{tr} P(B)\,\Sigma$. If $Q \neq I$, we may apply a transformation and define $\bar{B} = Q^{-\frac{1}{2}}B$, and $\bar{\Sigma} = Q^{\frac{1}{2}}\Sigma Q^{\frac{1}{2}}$; the r.h.s. of (3.3) then becomes $\operatorname{tr} Q^{\frac{1}{2}}\bar{B}(\bar{B}'\bar{B})^{-1}\bar{B}Q^{\frac{1}{2}}\Sigma = \operatorname{tr} \bar{B}(\bar{B}'\bar{B})^{-1}\bar{B}\bar{\Sigma} = \operatorname{tr} P(\bar{B})\bar{\Sigma}$, whereas the restrictions may be written as $\bar{h}(\bar{B}) = h(Q^{\frac{1}{2}}\bar{B}) = 0$. So without loss of generality we may take $Q = I$; we will do so henceforth.

The <u>sample</u> problem is now to estimate the population value Σ on the basis of a sample by a consistent, asymptotically normal estimator $\hat{\Sigma}_T$. The unconstrained problem has been treated by Van Praag (1983). For the sake of exposition we recapitulate the main result. Since the value of B, minimizing (3.3), is a function of Σ we may let $B(\Sigma)$ play the role of $\underset{\sim}{f}$ in Section 2. Then $\underset{\sim}{B}$ is consistently estimated by $B(\hat{\Sigma}_T)$ and $\sqrt{T}(B(\hat{\Sigma}_T) - B(\Sigma))$ is asymptotically normal.

In order to arrive at $B(\Sigma)$ we need the following theorem that we state without proof (cf. Rao (1973)):

<u>Theorem 1</u> Let P_0 be the orthogonal projection of R^k on the space spanned by the p minimal eigenvectors of Σ. Then $\operatorname{tr} P(B)\Sigma = \operatorname{tr} P(B)\,\Sigma\,P(B)$ is minimal if and only if $P(B) = P_0$.

Note that there are many matrices B with $P(B) = P_0$, so the minimizer of (3.3) is not unique. A natural choice for B is the following one. Let $B_1,\ldots,B_p$ be the p minimal eigenvectors of Σ, say $B_i\Sigma = \mu_i B_i$ $(i = 1,\ldots,p)$, and assume that the p eigenvalues all have multiplicity one. We may take $||B_i|| = 1$, for $i = 1,...,p$. Now define the matrix B by $B = [B_1',...,B_p']$. The theorem from Section 2 enables us to write down the asymptotic covariance matrix of $\sqrt{T}(\tilde{B}(\hat{\Sigma}_T) - \tilde{B}(\Sigma))$ as

$$\left(\frac{d\tilde{B}}{d\tilde{\Sigma}}\right) V \left(\frac{d\tilde{B}}{d\tilde{\Sigma}}\right)' , \tag{3.4}$$

where V is described in Section 2 and where the differential expression is given by $\frac{dB_i}{d\tilde{\Sigma}}(\Sigma) = -(\Sigma - \mu_i I)^+ (B_i \otimes I_k)$. Here $(\Sigma - \mu_i I)^+$ denotes the Moore-Penrose inverse of $(\Sigma - \mu_i I)$.

4. THE CASE OF EQUALITY CONSTRAINTS ON B

The problem of equality constraints on h(B) can now be dealt with by straightforward generalization of the result in the previous section. First, consider the population problem. The expression (3.3) with $Q = I$, that is $\operatorname{tr} P(B)\,\Sigma$, is minimized subject to the m equations-constraint $h(B) = 0$, where h is a twice-differentiable function in B, taking values in R^m. It is solved by the Lagrange method yielding solution(s) of the type $(B(\Sigma),\lambda(\Sigma))$ where $\lambda(\Sigma)$ is an m-vector of Lagrange multipliers.
The problem of estimating $(B(\Sigma),\lambda(\Sigma))$ is solved by replacing Σ by its consistent estimator $\hat{\Sigma}_T$. Then $(B(\hat{\Sigma}_T),\lambda(\hat{\Sigma}_T))$ is consistent and asymptotically normal; its covariance matrix is assessed by (2.1) where we now need an expression for $\begin{pmatrix} \frac{d\tilde{B}}{d\tilde{\Sigma}}(\Sigma) \\ \frac{d\lambda}{d\tilde{\Sigma}}(\Sigma) \end{pmatrix}$. Define the Lagrangian function

$$L(\Sigma,B,\lambda) = \operatorname{tr} P(B)\,\Sigma - \lambda h(B)' , \tag{4.1}$$

where $\lambda \in R^m$ is the vector of Lagrangian multipliers. Differentiation with respect to B and addition of the constraints yields the Lagrange-equations

$$\frac{\partial L}{\partial \tilde{B}}(\Sigma,B(\Sigma),\lambda(\Sigma)) = 0 \quad \text{and} \quad h(B(\Sigma)) = 0. \tag{4.2}$$

We shall denote their solution by $(B(\Sigma),\lambda(\Sigma))$. We will assume henceforth that B and λ are totally differentiable in Σ and that the gradient matrix $\frac{d\tilde{h}}{dB}(B(\Sigma))$ is of full rank m.

Now define the function $\tilde{f}$ by $\tilde{f}(\Sigma,B) = \frac{\partial \text{ tr } P(B)\ \Sigma}{\partial \tilde{B}}$, so $\tilde{f}(\Sigma,B)$ is a 1×pk row vector. From (4.1) we have

$$\frac{\partial^2 L}{\partial \tilde{\Sigma} \partial \tilde{B}} = \frac{\partial \tilde{f}}{\partial \tilde{\Sigma}} \tag{4.3}$$

and

$$\frac{\partial^2 L}{\partial \lambda \partial \tilde{B}} = -\left(\frac{dh}{d\tilde{B}}\right)' \tag{4.4}$$

when evaluated in (Σ,B,λ). From (4.2) we deduce (taking $\frac{d}{d\tilde{\Sigma}}$):

$$\frac{\partial^2 L}{\partial \tilde{\Sigma} \partial \tilde{B}} + \frac{\partial^2 L}{(\partial \tilde{B})^2} \frac{d\tilde{B}}{d\tilde{\Sigma}} + \frac{\partial^2 L}{\partial \lambda \partial \tilde{B}} \frac{d\lambda}{d\tilde{\Sigma}} = 0 \tag{4.5}$$

when evaluated in $(\Sigma,B(\Sigma),\lambda(\Sigma))$. Finally, from $h(B(\Sigma)) \equiv 0$ it follows that

$$\frac{dh}{d\tilde{B}} \frac{d\tilde{B}}{d\tilde{\Sigma}} = 0. \tag{4.6}$$

According to the theorem stated in Section 2, $\sqrt{T}((\tilde{B}(\hat{\Sigma}_T),\lambda(\hat{\Sigma}_T)) - (\tilde{B}(\Sigma),\lambda(\Sigma)))$ is asymptotically normal with mean zero and covariance matrix

$$\begin{pmatrix} V_{BB} & V_{B\lambda} \\ V_{\lambda B} & V_{\lambda\lambda} \end{pmatrix} = \begin{pmatrix} \frac{d\tilde{B}}{d\tilde{\Sigma}}(\Sigma) \\ \frac{d\lambda}{d\tilde{\Sigma}}(\Sigma) \end{pmatrix} V \left[\left(\frac{d\tilde{B}}{d\tilde{\Sigma}}(\Sigma)\right)' \ \left(\frac{d\lambda}{d\tilde{\Sigma}}(\Sigma)\right)' \right]. \tag{4.7}$$

Notice that the model specification determines the outer factors in (4.7) while the sample influence is only present in the middle factor. Notice also that $V_{B\lambda}$ does not need to be zero, which implies that $B(\hat{\Sigma}_T)$ and $\lambda(\hat{\Sigma}_T)$ are not stochastically independent (cf. Aitchison and Silvey (1958)).

Theorem 2 gives $\frac{d\tilde{B}}{d\tilde{\Sigma}}$ and $\frac{d\lambda}{d\tilde{\Sigma}}$.

<u>Theorem 2</u> Define the pk×pk matrix $U = -\frac{\partial^2 L}{(\partial \tilde{B})^2}(\Sigma,B(\Sigma),\lambda(\Sigma))$ and the m×pk matrix $W = \frac{dh}{d\tilde{B}}(B(\Sigma))$. If U is invertible and W is of full rank m, then

$$\frac{d\tilde{B}}{d\tilde{\Sigma}} = (U^{-1} - U^{-1}W'(WU^{-1}W')^{-1}WU^{-1}) \frac{\partial \tilde{f}}{\partial \tilde{\Sigma}}$$

and $$\frac{d\tilde{\lambda}}{d\Sigma} = ((WU^{-1}W')^{-1}WU^{-1}) \frac{\partial \tilde{f}}{\partial \Sigma}.$$

Proof

From (4.3) - (4.6) we have

$$\begin{bmatrix} U & W' \\ W & 0 \end{bmatrix} \begin{bmatrix} \frac{d\tilde{B}}{d\Sigma} \\ \frac{d\tilde{\lambda}}{d\Sigma} \end{bmatrix} = \begin{bmatrix} \frac{\partial \tilde{f}}{\partial \Sigma} \\ 0 \end{bmatrix}$$

Under the rank conditions of the theorem, the matrix $\begin{bmatrix} U & W' \\ W & 0 \end{bmatrix}$ is invertible with inverse (see for instance Maddala (1977))

$$\begin{bmatrix} U^{-1} - U^{-1}W'(WU^{-1}W')^{-1}WU^{-1} & U^{-1}W'(WU^{-1}W')^{-1} \\ (WU^{-1}W')^{-1}WU^{-1} & -(WU^{-1}W')^{-1} \end{bmatrix}.$$

Explicit expressions for U and $\frac{\partial \tilde{f}}{\partial \Sigma}$ are derived in Appendix 2.

It is well-known that the matrix $\begin{bmatrix} U & W' \\ W & 0 \end{bmatrix}$ may be invertible even if U is singular. For instance, if W is of full rank m and $yUy' < 0$ if $yW = 0$ $(y \neq 0)$, then $\begin{bmatrix} U & W' \\ W & 0 \end{bmatrix}$ is still invertible (cf. Barten, Kloek and Lempers (1969)).

If $\begin{bmatrix} U & W' \\ W & 0 \end{bmatrix}$ is not invertible, the following procedure is often applicable (cf. Silvey (1959)). Suppose W is of full rank m and U is of rank $pk-\ell$ with $\ell \leqq m$. Suppose W has a $\ell \times pk$ submatrix W_1 such that $U + W_1'W_1$ has full rank pk. Without loss of generality we may assume that $W = \begin{bmatrix} W_1 \\ W_2 \end{bmatrix}$. From (4.6) we have $W \frac{d\tilde{B}}{d\Sigma} = 0$, so we also have $W_1 \frac{d\tilde{B}}{d\Sigma} = 0$.

But then $$\begin{bmatrix} U + W_1'W_1 & W' \\ W & 0 \end{bmatrix} \begin{bmatrix} \frac{d\tilde{B}}{d\Sigma} \\ \frac{d\tilde{\lambda}}{d\Sigma} \end{bmatrix} = \begin{bmatrix} \frac{\partial \tilde{f}}{\partial \Sigma} \\ 0 \end{bmatrix},$$

and since the matrix $\begin{bmatrix} U + W_1'W_1 & W' \\ W & 0 \end{bmatrix}$ is invertible we may still express $\frac{d\tilde{B}}{d\Sigma}$ and $\frac{d\tilde{\lambda}}{d\Sigma}$ as a function of U,W and $\frac{\partial \tilde{f}}{d\Sigma}$.

5. CONCLUSIONS

In this paper we discussed the asymptotic distribution of the estimator $B(\hat{\Sigma}_T)$ under differentiable side-conditions $h(B) = 0$. The asymptotic distribution under no distributional assumptions, except the finiteness of the fourth-order moments of X is derived. In applications, the asymptotic covariance matrix (4.7) requires an evaluation in the point $(\hat{\Sigma}_T, B(\hat{\Sigma}_T), \lambda(\hat{\Sigma}_T))$ as is clear from the formulas derived in Appendix 2. In general this value will be found by a numerical optimization process. The attractiveness of the approach outlined in this paper is that no distributional assumptions are made, except for the finiteness of fourth-order moments. Recently, attention has risen to the development of methods that do not make the assumption of a random sample from a multivariate normal distribution. Bentler (1983) and Dijkstra (1983) discuss this topic in the context of the analyses of covariance structures. Dijkstra (1983) also discusses another relaxation of traditional assumptions, namely, the effect of incorrect restrictions on the parameter space. The method of population-sample decomposition, employed in this paper, may be generalized to other objective functions than tr $P(B)\,\Sigma$. The only two requirements are that the parameters are differentiable functions of some finite-order moments of X, and that the sample analogues of these moments are asymptotically normal.

Appendix 1. SOME ADDITIONAL NOTATIONS

Let $f : R^{n+m} \to R^k$ be a differentiable function, and let $z_0 = (x_0, y_0)$ be in R^{n+m}.
By $\frac{df}{dz}(z_0)$ we denote the derivative of f, evaluated in z_0. It is a $k\times(m+n)$ matrix. The partial derivatives of f are denoted by $\frac{\partial f}{\partial x}(x_0, y_0)$ and $\frac{\partial f}{\partial y}(x_0, y_0)$. If evaluation in $z_0 = (x_0, y_0)$ is clear from the context, we simply write $\frac{df}{dz}$, $\frac{\partial f}{\partial x}$ and $\frac{\partial f}{\partial y}$. If k=1 and f is twice differentiable, $\frac{\partial^2 f}{\partial y \partial x}$ is the $m\times n$ matrix with (i,j)-entry $\frac{\partial^2 f}{\partial y_j \partial x_i}$. Let g be a real valued matrix function, so $g(A) \in R$ for the $m\times n$ matrix A. By $\frac{dg}{dA}$ we denote the $m\times n$ matrix with (i,j)-entry $\frac{\partial g}{\partial a_{ij}}$, and by $\frac{dg}{d\underset{\sim}{A}}$ the $1\times mn$ matrix $(\text{vec}\,\frac{dg}{dA})'$.
If g is a matrix function, taking values in R^k, then $\frac{dg}{dA}$ is defined to be

the m×kn matrix $\left[\frac{dg_1}{dA} \; \cdots\cdots \; \frac{dg_k}{dA}\right]$.

By $\frac{d\tilde{g}}{dA}$ we denote the k×mn matrix

$$\begin{bmatrix} \frac{d\tilde{g}_1}{dA} \\ \cdot \\ \cdot \\ \cdot \\ \frac{d\tilde{g}_k}{dA} \end{bmatrix} .$$

Finally, if g(A) is a p×q matrix and A is a m×n matrix, then $\frac{dg}{dA}$ is the pm×qn matrix

$$\begin{bmatrix} \frac{dg_{11}}{dA} & \cdots\cdots\cdots\cdots & \frac{dg_{1q}}{dA} \\ \cdot & & \\ \cdot & & \\ \cdot & & \\ \frac{dg_{p1}}{dA} & & \frac{dg_{pq}}{dA} \end{bmatrix} ,$$

whereas the pq×mn matrix $\frac{d\tilde{g}}{dA}$ has $\frac{\partial g_{ij}}{\partial a_{rs}}$ as its ((j-1)p+i,(s-1)m+r) entry (i=1,...,p; j=1,...,q; r=1,...,m; s=1,...,n).

All these notations are adopted in order to be consistent with Balestra (1976). From Balestra we also define $P_{m,n}$ to be a matrix of order mn×mn, namely

$$P_{m,n} = \begin{bmatrix} S_{11} & S_{12} & \cdots\cdots & S_{1m} \\ S_{21} & & & \\ \cdot & & & \\ \cdot & & & \\ \cdot & & & \\ S_{n1} & \cdots\cdots\cdots\cdots & & S_{nm} \end{bmatrix} ,$$

where S_{ij} is a matrix of order m×n with 1 on the (i,j) entry and zero elsewhere.

Appendix 2.

In this section explicit expressions are derived for the matrices $\tilde{U}$ and $\frac{\partial \tilde{f}}{\partial \Sigma}$ from Section 4. We start with f(Σ,B). First note that tr P(B) Σ =

$\text{tr}\, \Sigma^{\frac{1}{2}} P(B)\, \Sigma^{\frac{1}{2}} = \text{tr}\, \Sigma^{\frac{1}{2}} B(B'B)^{-1} B'\Sigma^{\frac{1}{2}}$.

Balestra, formula (5.2.16) now gives

$$f(\Sigma,B) = \frac{\partial}{\partial B} (\text{tr}\, \Sigma^{\frac{1}{2}}B(B'B)^{-1}B'\Sigma^{\frac{1}{2}}) = 2\Sigma B(B'B)^{-1} - 2B(B'B)^{-1}B'\Sigma B(B'B)^{-1}.$$

Using Balestra, formulas (3.3.3) and (3.3.5) it follows that

$$\frac{\partial f}{\partial \Sigma} (\Sigma,B) = 2(\text{vec}\; I_k)(\text{vec}\; B(B'B)^{-1})' - 2(\text{vec}\; B(B'B)^{-1}B')(\text{vec}\; B(B'B)^{-1}).$$

From $\frac{\partial f}{\partial \Sigma}$ one may construct $\frac{\partial \tilde{f}}{\partial \Sigma}$ by using the fact that the $((i-1)k+r,$ $(j-1)k+s)$ entry of $\frac{\partial f}{\partial \Sigma}$ equals the $((j-1)k+i,(s-1)k+r)$ entry of $\frac{\partial \tilde{f}}{\partial \Sigma}$. It follows that $\frac{\partial \tilde{f}}{\partial \Sigma}$ is a $kp\times k^2$ matrix with

$$\frac{\partial f_{ij}}{\partial \sigma_{rs}} = 2\delta_{ir}[B(B'B)^{-1}]_{sj} - 2[B(B'B)^{-1}B']_{ir}\, [B(B'B)^{-1}]_{sj}$$

as its $((j-1)k+i,(s-1)k+r)$ entry, where δ_{ir} denotes the Kronecker delta $(j=1,\ldots,p;\; i,r,s=1,\ldots,k)$.

We will now derive an expression for U.

$$U = - \frac{\partial^2 L}{(\partial \tilde{B})^2} = - \frac{\partial \tilde{f}}{\partial \tilde{B}} + \sum_{i=1}^{m} \lambda_i \frac{d^2 h_i}{(d\tilde{B})^2} .$$

$$\text{Now } \frac{\partial f}{\partial B} = 2\, \frac{\partial \Sigma B(B'B)^{-1}}{\partial B} - 2\, \frac{\partial B(B'B)^{-1}B'\Sigma B(B'B)^{-1}}{\partial B} . \tag{A.1}$$

With Balestra, formulas (3.3.2) and (3.4.6) one gets

$$\frac{\partial \Sigma B(B'B)^{-1}}{\partial B} = (\Sigma \otimes I_k)(\text{vec}\; I_k)(\text{vec}\; I_p)'((B'B)^{-1} \otimes I_p) + (\Sigma B \otimes I_k)\, \frac{\partial (B'B)^{-1}}{\partial B} =$$

$$= (\Sigma \otimes I_k)(\text{vec}\; I_k)(\text{vec}\; I_p)'((B'B)^{-1} \otimes I_p) +$$

$$- (\Sigma B \otimes I_k)[P_{k,p}(B(B'B)^{-1} \otimes (B'B)^{-1}) + (\text{vec}\; B(B'B)^{-1})(\text{vec}\; (B'B)^{-1})'] =$$

$$= (\text{vec}\; \Sigma)(\text{vec}(B'B)^{-1})' - (\Sigma B \otimes I_k)[P_{k,p}(B(B'B)^{-1} \otimes (B'B)^{-1}) +$$

$$(\text{vec}\; B(B'B)^{-1})(\text{vec}(B'B)^{-1})']. \tag{A.2}$$

Next

$$\frac{\partial B(B'B)^{-1}B'\Sigma B(B'B)^{-1}}{\partial B} =$$

$$\frac{\partial B(B'B)^{-1}B'}{\partial B}(\Sigma B(B'B)^{-1} \otimes I_p) + (B(B'B)^{-1}B'\Sigma \otimes I_k)\frac{\partial B(B'B)^{-1}}{\partial B}.$$

Here

$$\frac{\partial B(B'B)^{-1}B'}{\partial B} = \frac{\partial B}{\partial B}((B'B)^{-1}B' \otimes I_p) + (B \otimes I_k)\frac{\partial (B'B)^{-1}}{\partial B}(B' \otimes I_p) +$$

$$+ (B(B'B)^{-1} \otimes I_k)\frac{\partial B'}{\partial B} =$$

$$(\text{vec } I_k)(\text{vec } I_p)'((B'B)^{-1}B' \otimes I_p) +$$

$$- (B \otimes I_k)[P_{k,p}(B(B'B)^{-1} \otimes (B'B)^{-1}) + (\text{vec } B(B'B)^{-1})$$

$$(\text{vec } (B'B)^{-1})'](B' \otimes I_p) + (B(B'B)^{-1} \otimes I_k)P_{k,p} .$$

For $\frac{\partial B(B'B)^{-1}}{\partial B}$, use (A.2) with $\Sigma = I_k$.

From $\frac{\partial f}{\partial B}$ one can easily construct $\frac{\partial \tilde{f}}{\partial \tilde{B}}$ since the $((j-1)k+i,(s-1)k+r)$ entry of $\frac{\partial \tilde{f}}{\partial \tilde{B}}$ equals the $((i-1)k+r,(j-1)p+s)$ entry of $\frac{\partial f}{\partial B}$, where $i,r = 1,\dots,k$ and $j,s = 1,\dots,p$.

REFERENCES

Aitchison, J. and D.S. Silvey (1958), "Maximum-likelihood estimation of parameters subject to restraints", Annals of Mathematical Statistics 29, pp.813-828.

Balestra, P. (1976), La Dérivation Matricielle, Sirey, Paris.

Barten, A.P., T. Kloek and F.B. Lempers (1969), "A note on a class of utility and production functions yielding everywhere differentiable demand functions", Review of Economic Studies 36, pp.109-111.

Bentler, P.M. (1983), "Simultaneous equation systems as moment structure models: with an introduction to latent variable models", Journal of Econometrics 22, pp.13-42.

Cramér, H. (1946), Mathematical Methods of Statistics, Princeton University, Princeton.

Dhrymes, Ph.J. (1970), Econometrics, Harper and Row, New York.

Dijkstra, T.K. (1983), "Some comments on maximum likelihood and partial least squares methods", Journal of Econometrics 22, pp.67-90.

Huber, P.J. (1981), Robust Statistics, Wiley, New York.

Intriligator, M.D. (1971), Mathematical Optimization and Economic Theory, Prentice-Hall, Englewood Cliffs.

Keller, W.J. and T. Wansbeek (1983), "Multivariate methods for quantitative and qualitative data", Journal of Econometrics 22, pp.91-111.

Lee, S.Y. and P.M. Bentler (1980), "Some asymptotic properties of constrained generalized least squares estimation in covariance structure models", South African Statistical Journal 14, pp.121-136.

Maddala, G.S. (1977), Econometrics, McGraw-Hill, Auckland.

Muirhead, R.J. (1982), Aspects of Multivariate Statistical Theory, Wiley, New York.

Pearson, K. (1901), "On lines and planes of closest fit to systems of points in space", Philosophical Magazine 2, pp.559-572.

Pollock, D.S.G. (1979), The Algebra of Econometrics, Wiley, New York.

Rao, C.R. (1973), Linear Statistical Inference and its Applications, Wiley, New York.

Silvey, D.S. (1959), "The Lagrangian multiplier test", Annals of Mathematical Statistics 30, pp.389-407.

Van Praag, B.M.S. (1983), "The Population-Sample Decompostion Approach", Report 82.18, Center for Research in Public Economics, Leyden University.

Van Praag, B.M.S., T.K. Dijkstra and J. Van Velzen (1984), "Least-squares theory based on general distributional assumptions with an application to the incomplete observations problem", Psychometrika, forthcoming.

Van Praag, B.M.S., T. Goedhart and A. Kapteyn (1980), "The poverty line in Europe - A pilot survey in Europe", Review of Economics and Statistics 63, pp.461-465.

White, H. (1980), "Nonlinear regression on cross-section data", Econometrica 48, pp.721-746.

White, H. (1982), "Maximum likelihood estimation of misspecified models", Econometrica 50, pp.1-25.

MEASUREMENT ERROR AND ENDOGENEITY IN REGRESSION: BOUNDS FOR ML AND 2SLS ESTIMATES

Paul Bekker*)
Arie Kapteyn
Tom Wansbeek

0. ABSTRACT

We consider the single equation errors in variables model and assume that a researcher is willing to specify upper bounds on the possible measurement errors in the exogenous variables. We prove that as a result the set of possible ML estimates is bounded by an ellipsoid. The result is generalized to IV estimation of a structural equation of a simultaneous system, which has only endogenous variables on the right hand side.

1. INTRODUCTION

In the presence of measurement error in the exogenous variables of a linear regression model, very little can be said in general about the true values of the regression parameter vector β. The situation changes when Ω, the measurement error covariance matrix, is known or can be estimated consistently. Then β can be estimated consistently and the asymptotic distribution of its estimator can be derived. This case has been discussed by various authors, including Schneeweiss (1976), Fuller (1980), Kapteyn and Wansbeek (1984).

An intermediate situation arises when Ω is not completely known and cannot be estimated consistently, but some prior knowledge is available. For this limited information case various procedures have been proposed. Blomqvist (1972) considers OLS and investigates its asymptotic bias as a function of the

*) Bekker and Kapteyn are with Tilburg University. Wansbeek is with the Netherlands Central Bureau of Statistics. The views expressed in this paper are those of the authors and do not necessarily reflect the policies of the CBS. Financial support by the Netherlands Organization for the Advancement of Pure Research (ZWO) is gratefully acknowledged.

size of the measurement error variance. In this approach, the researcher has to make a guess of Ω. If the computed asymptotic bias of the OLS-estimate is not too large, this is used as an indication that OLS can be used for estimation.

Hodges and Moore (1972) follow a similar approach but also develop a diagnostic for the sensitivity of the estimates to error in a particular observation. Davies and Hutton (1975) introduce a measure of "the distance from singularity" of the observed matrix of exogenous variables. To compute this measure one needs, once again, a guess of the size of the measurement errors in the exogenous variables. If the distance from singularity is small, the estimates are suspected to be unreliable. In a similar vein, Leamer (1983) presents "destructive diagnostics" which are "sets of measurement error variances compatible with the observed data which would imply that the true explanatory variables are perfectly collinear". In an empirical example, he concludes that even very small measurement errors in some explanatory variables would allow for the possibility of perfectly collinear explanatory variables.

Although it is true that generally one cannot say very much about the true value of β if Ω is unknown, there is a special case where the set of maximum likelihood estimates of β (under normality) can be bounded. This is the case where the measurement errors are uncorrelated and the k+1 estimates of β, obtained by regressing each of the k+1 variables involved (i.e. the one dependent variable and the k independent variables) on the remaining k variables, are all in the same orthant. Then the convex hull of the k+1 regressions contains all possible maximum likelihood estimates and any point in the hull is a possible maximum likelihood estimate. If the k+1 regressions are not all in the same orthant then the set of maximum likelihood estimates is unbounded. A proof of these results, as well as references to earlier work, can be found in Klepper and Leamer (1984).

For the case where the k+1 regressions are not in the same orthant, Klepper and Leamer (1984) introduce extra prior information which allows them to bound the set of maximum likelihood estimates. The prior information comes in two forms. Firstly, a researcher is supposed to be able to specify a maximum value of R^2 if all exogenous variables were measured accurately. It is shown that if this maximum is low enough, one can again bound the set of ML estimates by a convex hull. Secondly, a researcher is assumed to be able to give upper and lower bounds for the measurement error variances. If the upper bound is tight enough, so that the true explanatory variables cannot be perfectly collinear, the set of maximum likelihood estimates is shown to be bounded by an ellipsoid. In the derivation of the ellipsoid, based on a result in Leamer (1982), it is assumed that all exogenous variables are measured with error. Obviously, this is restrictive.

In Section 2 we generalize Klepper and Leamer's result to the case where some variables may be measured without error. Although we still arrive at an ellipsoid, the generalization is non-trivial. In practice, the most obvious use of the ellipsoid is based on extreme values of linear functions of the coefficients. These are derived in Section 3. We next consider, in Section 4, the possibility of jointly using the prior information on the covariance matrix of the measurement errors and on the maximum value of R^2. Our analysis suggests, however, that consistency of prior beliefs requires a maximum value of R^2 so high that it does not add information beyond the information implied by the prior beliefs about Ω.

In Section 5 we make a first attempt to generalize these results to a simultaneous equation setting where the exogenous variables may be measured with error. For a structural equation that contains only endogenous variables, we show that the set of consistent 2 SLS estimates is bounded by an ellipsoid.

Section 6 contains an empirical example. Section 7 concludes.

2. THE SINGLE EQUATION MODEL

Consider the single equation errors in variables model:

$$y = \Xi\beta + \varepsilon \tag{2.1}$$

$$X = \Xi + V, \tag{2.2}$$

where $\Xi(n\times k)$ is the matrix of true, but possibly unobservable, explanatory variables. The matrix $X(n\times k)$ contains the observations on Ξ whilst $V(n\times k)$ contains the measurement errors. The vector $y(n\times 1)$ contains the observations of the endogenous variables and $\varepsilon(n\times 1)$ is a vector of random errors satisfying $E\varepsilon=0$, $E\varepsilon\varepsilon'=\sigma^2 I_n$. Let v_i' be the i-th row of V, then we assume $Ev_i=0$, $Ev_i v_i'=\Omega$, $E\varepsilon v_i'=0$, $i=1,\ldots,n$, and $Ev_i v_j'=0$ for $i\neq j$. We assume both ε and the elements of V to be normally distributed and uncorrelated with Ξ.

Define the k×k-matrix $A \equiv \frac{1}{n}X'X$. If we assume that the elements of Ξ are also drawings from a normal distribution and Ω is known, then the ML estimate of β is the solution of the following moments equation:

$$(A-\Omega)\beta = \frac{1}{n}X'y \equiv r \tag{2.3}$$

(for notational simplicity we use the same symbol for β and for its maximum likelihood estimate as long as no confusion can arise). If we assume that the elements of Ξ are constants and that $\frac{1}{n}\Xi'\Xi$ converges to a finite limit for $n \to \infty$, then the solution of (2.3) is still a consistent estimate of the regression parameters (e.g., Kapteyn and Wansbeek, 1984).

We assume that, although Ω is unknown, the researcher is willing to specify bounds within which Ω must lie, i.e.

$$0 \leqslant \Omega \leqslant \Omega^{*} \tag{2.4}$$

with Ω^{*} specified by the researcher. We assume that Ω^{*} is symmetric and that it satisfies

$$0 \leqslant \Omega^{*} < A. \tag{2.5}$$

This assumption prevents the possibility of $A-\Omega$ being singular, a case discussed extensively by Leamer (1983).

For what follows, the following lemma is useful. The symbol "+" denotes the Moore-Penrose inverse of a matrix; the notation $C \leq D$ is used to indicate that $D-C$ is a positive semi-definite matrix; $C < D$ means $D-C$ is positive definite.

Lemma 1. Let C and C^{*} be symmetric matrices; then

$$0 \leqslant C \leqslant C^{*} \tag{2.6}$$

is equivalent with

$$C^{*}C^{*+}C = C \quad \& \quad C \geqslant CC^{*+}C \quad \& \quad C^{*} \geq 0. \tag{2.7}$$

Proof: Diagonalize C^* as follows

$$C^* = (P_1,P_2)\begin{pmatrix}\Phi & 0\\ 0 & 0\end{pmatrix}\begin{pmatrix}P_1'\\ P_2'\end{pmatrix} = P_1\Phi P_1' , \tag{2.8}$$

with Φ diagonal and nonsingular, $P_1'P_1 = I$, $P_2'P_2 = I$, $P_1'P_2 = 0$. Define $H \equiv P_1'CP_1$ and let Q diagonalize both Φ and H: $Q'\Phi Q = I$, $Q'HQ = D$, with D diagonal.

(i) If $0 \leq C \leq C^*$, then $0 \leq P_2'CP_2 \leq P_2'C^*P_2 = 0$, so $P_2'C = 0$. Consequently C lies in the space spanned by the columns of P_1. As P_1P_1' projects onto this space, $P_1P_1'C = C$. Since $C^*C^{*+} = P_1\Phi P_1'P_1\Phi^{-1}P_1 = P_1P_1'$, we have $C^*C^{*+}C = C$. Furthermore, $0 \leq Q'P_1'CP_1Q \leq Q'P_1'C^*P_1Q = I$, so $0 \leq D \leq I$. Thus $C-CC^{x+}C =$ $= P_1HP_1' - P_1H\phi^{-1}HP_1' = P_1Q'^{-1}(D-D^2)Q^{-1}P_1' \geq 0$.

(ii) If $C^*C^{*+}C = P_1P_1'C = C$, then $C = P_1P_1'CP_1P_1' = P_1HP_1'$. If, moreover, $C - CC^{*+}C = P_1Q'^{-1}(D-D^2)Q^{-1}P_1' \geq 0$, then $D - D^2 \geq 0$ or $0 \leq D \leq I$. Hence $0 \leq P_1Q'^{-1}DQ^{-1}P_1' \leq P_1Q'^{-1}Q^{-1}P_1'$ or $0 \leq C \leq C^*$, Q.E.D.

Corollary 1. Let x be a vector and C^* a symmetric matrix, then

$$xx' \leq C^* \tag{2.9}$$

is equivalent with

$$C^*C^{*+}x = x \quad \& \quad x'C^{*+}x \leq 1 \quad \& \quad C^* \geq 0. \tag{2.10}$$

Proof: Use Lemma 1 with $C = xx'$ and note that $C^*C^{*+}xx' = xx'$ is equivalent with $C^*C^{*+}x = x$ and $xx' \geq xx'C^{*+}xx'$ is equivalent with $x'C^{*+}x \leq 1$, Q.E.D.

The main result of this section is contained in Proposition 1. The following symbols are used:

$$F^* \equiv (A-\Omega^*)^{-1} - A^{-1} \tag{2.11}$$

$$b^* \equiv (A-\Omega^*)^{-1}r \tag{2.12}$$

$$b \equiv A^{-1}r. \tag{2.13}$$

Proposition 1. <u>The set of solutions</u> β <u>satisfying</u> (2.3), <u>with</u> Ω and Ω^* satisfying (2.4) and (2.5), <u>is given by</u>

$$(\beta-b^*)'F^{*+}(\beta-b) \leq 0 \quad \& \quad F^*F^{*+}(\beta-b) = \beta-b. \tag{2.14}$$

<u>Conversely, for any</u> β <u>satisfying</u> (2.14) <u>there exists an</u> Ω <u>such that</u> (2.3) <u>and</u> (2.4) <u>hold true</u>.

<u>Proof</u>:

(i) Define $F \equiv (A-\Omega)^{-1} - A^{-1}$, so that $0 \leq F \leq F^*$, $\beta - b = FAb$, $b^* - b = F^*Ab$, and $\beta - b^* = (F-F^*)Ab$. Lemma 1 implies

$$FF^{*+}F - F \leq 0 \ \& \ F^*F^{*+}F = F. \tag{2.15}$$

So

$$(F-F^*)F^{*+}F \leq 0 \ \& \ F^*F^{*+}FAb = FAb. \tag{2.16}$$

Hence

$$b'A(F-F^*)F^{*+}FAb \leq 0 \ \& \ F^*F^{*+}(\beta-b) = \beta - b \tag{2.17}$$

or

$$(\beta-b^*)'F^{*+}(\beta-b) \leq 0 \ \& \ F^*F^{*+}(\beta-b) = \beta - b. \tag{2.18}$$

(ii) To prove the converse we pick an arbitrary β satisfying (2.14) and construct an F (of rank one) which satisfies (2.3) and (2.15). For F we choose

$$\tilde{F} = \frac{(\beta-b)(\beta-b)'}{b'A(\beta-b)}, \tag{2.19}$$

if $\beta \neq b$, and $\tilde{F} = 0$ if $\beta = b$; $\tilde{F}$ satisfies $\beta - b = \tilde{F}Ab$, so that (2.3) holds true. Using Corollary 1, we know that $\tilde{F}$ satisfies (2.15) if

$$(\beta-b)'F^{*+}(\beta-b) \leq (\beta-b)'Ab \quad \& \quad F^*F^{*+}(\beta-b) = \beta - b \tag{2.20}$$

where we have used the fact that $b'A(\beta-b) = \beta'(A-\Omega)\beta - \beta'(A-\Omega)A^{-1}(A-\Omega)\beta$ is positive if $\beta \neq b$.

The second part of (2.20) is simply the second part of (2.14). Next, using this fact, we can also see that the first part of (2.20) is equivalent with the first part of (2.20). For, the first part of (2.20) can be written as

$$(\beta-b)'[F^{*+}(\beta-b) - F^{*+}F^{*}Ab] \leq 0. \tag{2.21}$$

Using $F^{*}Ab = b^{*} - b$ this is equivalent with

$$(\beta-b)'F^{*+}(\beta-b^{*}) \leq 0, \tag{2.22}$$

which is the first part of (2.14), Q.E.D.

Note that (2.14) can be rewritten as

$$(\beta-\tfrac{1}{2}(b+b^{*}))'F^{*+}(\beta-\tfrac{1}{2}(b+b^{*})) \leq \tfrac{1}{4}(b^{*}-b)'F^{*+}(b^{*}-b) \;\; \& \tag{2.23}$$

$$F^{*}F^{*+}[\beta - \tfrac{1}{2}(b+b^{*})] = \beta - \tfrac{1}{2}(b+b^{*}). \tag{2.24}$$

(2.23) represents a cylinder, so that (2.23) and (2.24) represent the ellipsoid that is obtained by projecting the cylinder orthogonally onto the space spanned by F^{*}.

For the case that there are measurement errors in all variables, i.e. Ω^{*} is nonsingular, (2.24) turns into an identity and (2.23) becomes an ellipsoid with $F^{*+} = F^{*-1}$. This special case has been given before by Klepper and Leamer (1984). The midpoint of the ellipsoid is $\frac{1}{2}(b+b^{*})$, which is the "compromise" between the two extreme cases b ($\Omega = 0$) and b^{*} ($\Omega = \Omega^{*}$).

Given that we started from an inequality condition on Ω rather than F it might seem more obvious to derive an ellipsoid in terms of Ω^{*+} rather than F^{*+}. This can indeed be done and the result is equivalent to Proposition 1. We state this as Proposition 2.

<u>Proposition 2. The set of solutions</u> β <u>satisfying</u> (2.3), <u>with</u> Ω <u>satisfying</u> (2.4), <u>is given by</u>

$$(\beta-b^{*})'(A-\Omega^{*})\Omega^{*+}A(\beta-b) \leq 0 \quad \& \quad \Omega^{*}\Omega^{*+}A(\beta-b) = A(\beta-b). \tag{2.25}$$

Conversely, for any β satisfying (2.25) there exists an Ω such that (2.3) and (2.4) hold true. Furthermore, (2.14) and (2.25) are equivalent.

Proof: The proof is analogous to the proof of Proposition 1 and is therefore omitted.

Klepper and Leamer (1984) also consider a *lower* bound on Ω. We do not explicitly deal with this restriction, as any (non-zero) lower bound can be subtracted from A, and the analysis carries through with the thus adjusted A instead of A proper; so this extension is trivial.

3. EXTREME VALUES OF LINEAR FUNCTIONS OF β

If the number of regressors in (2.1) is larger than two it will be hard in practice to present the ellipsoid given by (2.23) and (2.24) in a transparent way. For that reason it is useful to derive bounds for linear functions of β. Let ψ be a known vector, then bounds for ψ'β are given by the following proposition.

Proposition 3. The maximum and minimum $\widehat{\psi\beta}$ *of* ψ'β, *with* ψ *fixed and* β *satisfying* (2.23) *and* (2.24), *are given by*

$$\psi'\hat{\beta} = \tfrac{1}{2}\psi'(b+b^*) \pm \tfrac{1}{2}\{(b^*-b)'Ab.\psi'F^*\psi\}^{\frac{1}{2}}. \tag{3.1}$$

Proof: Define

$$f \equiv \tfrac{1}{2}(b+b^*) \tag{3.2}$$

$$r^2 \equiv \tfrac{1}{4}(b^*-b)'F^{*+}(b^*-b) = \tfrac{1}{4}(b^*-b)'Ab, \tag{3.3}$$

and let $P_1\Phi P_1'$ be the singular value decomposition of F^* (so, $F^{*+} = P_1\Phi_1^{-1}P_1'$ and $P_1P_1' = F^*F^{*+}$). Thus the ellipsoid can be written as

$$(\beta-f)'F^{*+}(\beta-f) \leq r^2 \quad \& \quad P_1P_1'(\beta-f) = \beta-f. \tag{3.4}$$

Clearly, the extreme values of $\psi'\beta$ will be obtained for β on the ellipsoid and not in it. We find the extreme values by differentiating the Lagrangean function

$$\psi'\beta - \tfrac{1}{2}\lambda\{(\beta-f)'F^{*+}(\beta-f) - r^2\} + \mu'\{(I-P_1P_1')(\beta-f)\} \tag{3.5}$$

with respect to β, λ and μ and setting the derivatives equal to zero. This yields

$$\psi - \lambda F^{*+}(\beta-f) + (I-P_1P_1')\,\mu = 0 \tag{3.6}$$

and (3.4) (with the first part being an equality). Premultiply (3.6) by $\Phi^{\frac{1}{2}}P_1'$ to obtain

$$\lambda\Phi^{-\frac{1}{2}}P_1'(\beta-f) = \Phi^{\frac{1}{2}}P_1'\psi. \tag{3.7}$$

Squaring both sides yields $\lambda^2 r^2 = \psi'P_1'\Phi P_1'\psi$, so that $\lambda = \pm\{\psi'F^*\psi/r^2\}^{\frac{1}{2}}$. Next, we have from (3.6) premultipled by P_1P_1' that $F^{*+}(\beta-f) = P_1P_1'\psi/\lambda$, so (2.24) implies

$$\hat{\beta} = f \pm F^*\psi/\{\psi'F^*\psi/r^2\}^{\frac{1}{2}} \tag{3.8}$$

and the corresponding values of $\psi'\hat{\beta}$ as in (3.1) follow directly, Q.E.D.

4. AN EXTRA RESTRICTION

So far, we have ignored one piece of information a researcher may want to take into account, namely that errors in the equation have a non-negative variance σ^2. For a given Ω the ML estimate $\hat{\sigma}^2$ of σ^2, under normality of all variables, is

$$\hat{\sigma}^2 = \frac{1}{n}\,y'y - \beta'(A-\Omega)\beta = s^2 - \beta'\Omega b, \tag{4.1}$$

where $s^2 \equiv \frac{1}{n}\,y'y - b'Ab$, the usual residual variance estimator of σ^2 if there are no measurement errors. It seems reasonable to restrict the values of β to the set which generates non-negative values of $\hat{\sigma}^2$. Following Klepper and Leamer (1984) we allow for the possibility that a researcher "knows" that σ^2 not only is non-negative but actually is greater than or equal to some positive lower bound a, i.e. β should be such that $\hat{\sigma}^2 \geq a > 0$.

Using $\Omega\beta = A(\beta-b)$, $\hat{\sigma}^2 \geq a$ implies

$$(\beta-b)'Ab \leq s^2 - a. \tag{4.2}$$

So the admissible values of β have to be on one side of a hyperplane. Figure 1 presents a drawing of the ellipsoid defined by (2.23) and (2.24) in the space spanned by F^*. The area to the left of the solid straight line is where (4.2) is satisfied. In the shaded area (2.23), (2.24) and (4.2) hold simultaneously. It is easy to show furthermore that the planes tangent to the ellipsoid in b and b^* are parallel to the plane defined by $(\beta-b)'Ab = s^2 - a$. All three planes are orthogonal to the vector Ab.

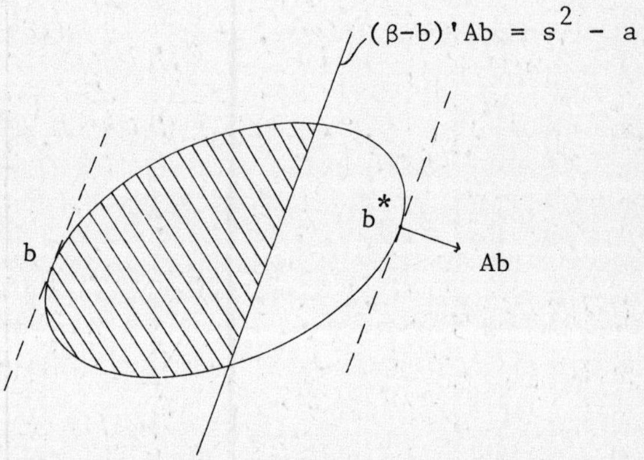

Figure 1. Feasible area for β.

Evidently, the restriction $\hat{\sigma}^2 \geq a$ can be ignored if $(\beta-b)'Ab = s^2 - a$ runs through the point b^* or if it is to the right of this point. For the plane to go through b^* there has to hold $(b^*-b)'Ab = s^2 - a$. Since $Ab = (A-\Omega)b^*$ there has to hold $b^{*\prime}\Omega b = s^2 - a$. From (4.1) it is clear that σ^{*2} (the estimate of σ^2 corresponding to Ω^*) is then equal to a. Thus, if $\sigma^{*2} \geq a$, the restriction $\hat{\sigma}^2 \geq a$ does not interfere with the ellipsoid, and it can be ignored.

The condition $\sigma^{*2} \geq a$ translates into a condition on Ω^*. An illuminating way of looking at it is the following one. Consider model (2.1) and the corresponding matrix of second order sample moments, adjusted for a:

$$B \equiv \begin{pmatrix} \frac{1}{n} y'y-a & \frac{1}{n} y'\Xi \\ \frac{1}{n} \Xi'y & \frac{1}{n} \Xi'\Xi \end{pmatrix} . \tag{4.3}$$

In view of (2.1), believing that the variance of ε is at least equal to a, also means that, at least asymptotically, the matrix B is positive semi-definite. The matrix B is unobservable, but we can construct another matrix C which, under general conditions, will converge in probability to the same matrix if $n \to \infty$:

$$C \equiv \begin{pmatrix} \frac{1}{n} y'y-a & \frac{1}{n} y'X \\ \frac{1}{n} X'y & A - \Omega \end{pmatrix} . \tag{4.4}$$

Given that B is positive semi-definite and that B - C converges in probability to zero if $n \to \infty$, it seems reasonable to impose the inequality

$$C^* \equiv \begin{pmatrix} \frac{1}{n} y'y-a & \frac{1}{n} y'X \\ \frac{1}{n} X'y & A - \Omega^* \end{pmatrix} \geqslant 0 \tag{4.5}$$

as a consistency requirement for a researcher's prior beliefs - after all, the whole analysis is in terms of asymptotic properties of estimates. This guarantees the positive semi-definiteness of C for any choice of Ω satisfying (2.3). Since we have already imposed the condition $A - \Omega^* > 0$, (4.5) amounts to $|C^*| \geqslant 0$. From the formula for the determinant of a partitioned matrix we know that

$$|C^*| = |A - \Omega^*| . \{\frac{1}{n} y'y - a - \frac{1}{n} y'X(A-\Omega^*)^{-1} \frac{1}{n} X'y\} \tag{4.6}$$

so that $C^* \geqslant 0$ is equivalent with

$$\frac{1}{n} y'y-a - \frac{1}{n} y'X(A-\Omega^*)^{-1} \frac{1}{n} X'y \geqslant 0 \tag{4.7}$$

or

$$\frac{1}{n} y'y - b'(A-\Omega^*)b \geqslant a. \tag{4.8}$$

From (4.1) it is clear that (4.8) is equivalent to the condition $\sigma^{*2} \geq a$.

Thus, if a researcher finds it reasonable to replace condition (2.5) by (4.5), then the condition $\hat{\sigma}^2 \geq a$ is satisfied automatically.

5. SIMULTANEOUS EQUATIONS

If the exogenous variables in a simultaneous system are subject to error, the 2SLS estimator of the structural parameters will generally be inconsistent. If the covariance matrix of the measurement errors is known, it is easy to adjust the 2SLS estimator so that it will be consistent (See Ketellapper, 1982, for details). Consider the j-th structural equation:

$$y_j = Y_j\alpha + \Xi_j\gamma + \varepsilon_j \tag{5.1}$$

$$X = \Xi + V \; ; \tag{5.2}$$

Y_j and Ξ_j are matrices of endogenous and exogenous variables, respectively, included in this equation, Ξ is the matrix of all exogenous variables measured by X; ε_j and V have the same properties as in Section 2, but in addition V is independent of Y_j. The covariance matrix of the rows of V is once again called Ω.

Ketellapper (1982) gives the following adjustment of 2SLS as a consistent estimate of α and γ:

$$\begin{pmatrix} \hat{\alpha} \\ \hat{\gamma} \end{pmatrix} = \begin{pmatrix} Y_j'X(X'X-n.\Omega)^{-1}X'Y_j & Y_j'X_j \\ X_j'Y_j & X_j'X_j-n.\Omega_j \end{pmatrix}^{-1} \cdot \begin{pmatrix} Y'X(X'X-n.\Omega)^{-1}X'y_j \\ X_j'y_j \end{pmatrix} \tag{5.3}$$

where Ω_j is the submatrix of Ω corresponding to Ξ_j.

Analogous to Section 2, it would be nice to postulate bounds for Ω and derive bounds for $\hat{\alpha}$ and $\hat{\gamma}$. At this moment we only have results for a structural equation with endogenous variables only, i.e. where $\gamma \equiv 0$. In that case (5.3) reduces to (omitting the subscript j and the caret over α):

$$\alpha = \left(\frac{Y'X}{n} (A-\Omega)^{-1} \frac{X'Y}{n} \right)^{-1} \frac{Y'X}{n} (A-\Omega)^{-1} \frac{X'y}{n} \,, \tag{5.4}$$

with $A \equiv \frac{1}{n} X'X$, as before.

Assume once again that a researcher is able to specify a matrix Ω^* such that (2.4) and (2.5) hold true. Then we will show that the set of all α's satis-fying (5.4) with all Ω's satisfying (2.4) is bounded by an ellipsoid. It is easy to see, however, that in contrast with the regression case, all α's in this set are consistent estimates of the corresponding true parameter vector as long as we maintain the assumption that V and ε are independent. This is so because the equation under consideration only involves endogenous variables.

Since all α's are consistent, the ellipsoid shrinks to zero for $n \to \infty$. Still, in finite samples, different choices of Ω will yield different estimates. Therefore, it remains of interest to see how estimates vary with the choice of assumptions.

The derivation of the ellipsoid rests on two steps. First we rewrite (5.4) in a form which allows us to use Proposition 1 and then we transform this ellipsoid back into a form that allows us to make direct inferences about α.

To carry out the first step we need some notation. Let

$$R \equiv \frac{1}{n} X'(y,Y), \tag{5.5}$$

then (5.4) can be written as

$$R'(A-\Omega)^{-1}R\binom{-1}{\alpha} = \binom{-\delta}{0}, \tag{5.6}$$

where

$$\delta \equiv \frac{1}{n} y'X(A-\Omega)^{-1} \frac{1}{n} X'y - \alpha'\{\frac{1}{n} Y'X(A-\Omega)^{-1} \frac{1}{n} X'Y\}\alpha. \tag{5.7}$$

For later reference, notice that $\delta \geq 0$. Furthermore, according to (5.1) we have that $X'y = X'Y\alpha + X'\varepsilon$ so that under quite general assumptions $\delta > 0$ with probability one, but also that δ converges to zero in probability if $n \to \infty$. Define

$$F \equiv \{R'A^{-1}R\}^{-1} - \{R'(A-\Omega)^{-1}R\}^{-1} \tag{5.8}$$

$$F^* \equiv \{R'A^{-1}R\}^{-1} - \{R'(A-\Omega^*)^{-1}R\}^{-1} \tag{5.9}$$

$$\beta \equiv \frac{1}{\delta}\binom{-1}{\alpha} = -\left\{R'(A-\Omega)^{-1}R\right\}^{-1} e_1 \tag{5.10}$$

with e_1 being the first unit vector,

$$b \equiv -\left\{R'A^{-1}R\right\}^{-1} e_1 \tag{5.11}$$

$$b^* \equiv -\left\{R'(A-\Omega^*)^{-1}R\right\}^{-1} e_1. \tag{5.12}$$

Thus we have

$$0 \leq F \leq F^*,\ \beta - b = Fe_1,\ b^* - b = F^*e_1. \tag{5.13}$$

Comparison with the definitions used in the proof of Proposition 1 makes it clear that β satisfies the conditions of Proposition 1, i.e. the set of estimates β is confined by

$$(\beta-b^*)'F^{*+}(\beta-b) \leq 0 \quad \& \quad F^*F^{*+}(\beta-b) = \beta - b. \tag{5.14}$$

This concludes the first step.

The second step is to transform the ellipsoid for β into an ellipsoid for α. At this moment we are only able to do this for the case where F^* is non-singular, i.e. $\Omega^* > 0$. The result is given in Proposition 4.

Proposition 4. For F^* non-singular α satisfies

$$\left\{\binom{-1}{\alpha}' F^{*-1}\left(\frac{b+b^*}{2}\right)\right\}^2 - \left\{\binom{-1}{\alpha}' F^{*-1}\binom{-1}{\alpha}\right\}.b^{*'}F^{*-1}b \geq 0. \tag{5.15}$$

Proof: Substitute $\frac{1}{\delta}\binom{-1}{\alpha}$ for β in the first part of (5.14). This gives a quadratic inequality in δ^{-1}. The quadratic expression in δ^{-1} describes a parabola. For the inequality to hold, the parabola has to intersect the abscissa at least once. This requires the discriminant of the quadratic expression to be non-negative. This is (5.15). Thus (5.15) provides a necessary condition for α, Q.E.D.

6. AN EMPIRICAL EXAMPLE

In Van de Stadt, Kapteyn, Van de Geer (1983) (SKG from now on) a model of preference formation is constructed and estimated. The central relationship of the model is the following one

$$\mu_i = \beta_0 + \beta_1\mu_i(-1) + \beta_2 fs_i(-1) + \beta_3 fs_i + \beta_4 y_i + \beta_5 y_i^* + \beta_6 fs_i^* + \varepsilon_i. \quad (6.1)$$

The index i refers to the i-th household in the sample; μ_i is a measure of the household's present wants (exp (μ_i) is the income the household head would consider "just about sufficient to make ends meet"); $\mu_i(-1)$ is the same measure observed one year ago for the same household; fs_i is the log of the present number of household members ("log-family size") whereas $fs_i(-1)$ is log-family size one year ago; y_i is the present after tax household log-income. The starred variables are sample means of log-incomes and log-family sizes in "the social group" to which household i belongs. A social group is a set of households with identical characteristics (the age of the household head is in the same age bracket, the household heads have a similar education and they live in a town of similar size); ε_i is a random disturbance term. See SKG for further details.

Thus relation (6.1) explains the level of a household's present financial wants by its familiy size (both present and lagged one period), its present log income (habit formation), by present log income and log-family size in the household's social group (preference interdependence), and by the level of financial wants one year ago (habit formation).

Since ε_i is allowed to show negative serial correlation (this follows from the theory underlying (6.1) - see SKG), $\mu_i(-1)$ may correlate negatively with ε_i. This is equivalent to allowing a measurement error in $\mu_i(-1)$. The variables y_i^* and f_i^* are proxies for reference group effects and may therefore be expected to suffer from measurement error; fs_i and $fs_i(-1)$ are crude proxies of the effects of family composition on financial wants, which can therefore also be expected to suffer from measurement error. Finally, y_i may be subject to measurement error as well.

The sample means, variances and covariances of all variables involved are given in Table 1. Our specification of Ω^* is given in Table 2. The column headed "% error" indicates the standard deviation of the measurement errors (the square root of the diagonal of Ω^*) as a percentage of the sample standard deviation of the corresponding observed variables. So we allow, for example, a 40% measurement error in y_i^* and fs_i^*. These values are true a priori values in the sense that we have stuck to our first choice of Ω^* and not adjusted Ω^* after looking at the corresponding ellipsoid. Regarding the off-diagonal elements of Ω^* it should be noted that these values are not upper bounds for the corresponding elements of Ω. In Ω^* the block corresponding to $fs_i(-1)$ and fs_i is singular. This implies that in any Ω satisfying $0 \leq \Omega \leq \Omega^*$ the corresponding block will be singular as well. So we impose a perfect correlation in measurement error between both variables.

Table 1. Sample means and covariances of the observed variables.

Variable	Mean	Covariance with						
		μ_i	$\mu_i(-1)$	$fs_i(-1)$	fs_i	y_i	y_i^*	fs_i^*
μ_i	10.11	.1260						
$\mu_i(-1)$	10.07	.1123	.1348					
$fs_i(-1)$	1.01	.0876	.0922	.2706				
fs_i	1.00	.0887	.0889	.2559	.2751			
y_i	10.31	.1238	.1212	.0881	.0924	.1783		
y_i^*	10.30	.0606	.0593	.0523	.0533	.0782	.0828	
fs_i^*	1.00	.0434	.0443	.0873	.0880	.0515	.0535	.0972

Table 2. Value of Ω^*.

Variable	$\mu_i(-1)$	$fs_i(-1)$	fs_i	y_i	y_i^*	fs_i^*	% error
$\mu_i(-1)$	0.0219						40
$fs_i(-1)$		0.0061	0.0061				15
fs_i		0.0061	0.0061				15
y_i				0.0040			15
y_i^*					0.013	0.010	40
fs_i^*					0.010	0.015	40

Obviously, it is a little hard to present the ellipsoid in 5-dimensional space implied by (2.25). So we only present b, b^* and the extreme values of β obtained from (3.1) by choosing for ψ the six unit vectors successively. The results are given in Table 3. In the right-hand part of the table, the extreme values are on the diagonal and are underlined for clarity; the other entries in a row are the corresponding values for the other coefficients.

Table 3. Extreme Values of β.

	$b^{1)}$	b^*	choices for $\psi^{2)}$					
			e_1	e_2	e_3	e_4	e_5	e_6
β_1	0.509	0.950	0.968	0.505	0.928	0.515	0.689	0.745
	(0.026)		0.491	0.954	0.531	0.944	0.771	0.715
β_2	-0.013	-0.123	-0.128	-0.004	-0.107	-0.011	-0.063	-0.090
	(0.032)		-0.008	-0.132	-0.029	-0.125	-0.072	-0.046
β_3	0.066	0.116	0.119	0.070	0.125	0.064	0.089	0.077
	(0.031)		0.062	0.112	0.057	0.118	0.093	0.105
β_4	0.298	0.044	0.026	0.315	0.045	0.331	0.131	0.155
	(0.031)		0.315	0.027	0.297	0.010	0.210	0.186
β_5	0.072	0.028	0.024	0.060	0.041	0.013	0.197	0.034
	(0.029)		0.075	0.039	0.058	0.086	-0.098	0.065
β_6	-0.032	-0.020	-0.018	-0.061	-0.067	-0.035	-0.036	0.081
	(0.025)		-0.032	0.011	-0.017	-0.015	-0.014	-0.131

1) Standard errors (from OLS on (6.1) under OLS assumptions) in parentheses.

2) Each cell contains two values of $\hat{\beta}$, corresponding to the plus and the minus sign in (3.1) respectively. Given the choices for ψ, the i-th diagonal cell (i=1,...,6) contains the extreme values for β_i.

Comparison of b and b^* shows no sign reversals and also in the right hand side part of Table 3 only a few sign reversals occur. All sign reversals pertain to the social group variables y_i^* and fs_i^*. Thus it is possible to vary the assumptions in such a way that the estimates would indicate a negative effect of social group income on the financial wants of household i or a positive influence of the family size in the social group. Of course y_i^* and fs_i^* are the variables for which we have allowed the largest measurement variances. To prevent such outcomes one should be prepared to put tighter bounds on Ω.

The information conveyed by the extreme values of the estimates is quite different from the story told by the standard errors of the OLS estimates. For example, b_5 is about two and half times its standard error and b_3 about two times. Still the estimate of β_5 can switch signs, but the estimate of β_3 cannot. Combining the information obtained from the standard errors with the results of the sensitivity analysis suggests that β_1, β_3 and β_4 are unambiguously positive; β_2 does not reverse signs in the sensitivity analysis but the standard error of b_2 suggests that β_2 could be positive; b_5 has a relatively small standard error but the estimate of β_5 turns out to be sensitive to the choice of assumptions; b_6 has a relatively large standard error, and the estimate of β_6 is sensitive to the choice of assumptions.

7. CONCLUSION

We have generalized a result by Klepper and Leamer (1984) and made a first attempt to deal with simultaneous equations estimation in the presence of measurement error in exogenous variables. The models dealt with so far are rather simple. The issue of systematically investigating the sensitivity of estimates to stochastic assumptions (in this case the presence and size of measurement errors) is even more important in complicated models like the ones usually analyzed by means of the well-known LISREL program (cf. Jöreskog and Sörbom, 1981).

In our experience, estimates of structural parameters may sometimes change dramatically as a result of seemingly innocuous changes in the stochastic specification of the model. Given that the LISREL program is so widely used and in view of the wide variety of stochastic specifications it can deal with, it is important to understand how estimates change if we vary assumptions. If we do not have a clear understanding of the relation between data, assumptions and results, empirical work will not learn us very much about reality. To the extent that computer software becomes a black box (not because algorithms would be unknown, but because we do not fully understand how specification affects results), obtaining empirical results becomes an act of magic. Systematic sensitivity analysis is an important tool to help empirical researchers avoid the fate of the sorcerer's apprentice.

REFERENCES

Blomqvist, A.G. (1972), "Approximating the Least-Squares Bias in Multiple Regression with Errors in Variables", The Review of Economics and Statistics 54, 202-204.

Davies, R.B. and B. Hutton (1975), "The Effect of Errors in the Independent Variables in Linear Regression", Biometrika 62, 383-391.

Fuller, W.A. (1980), "Properties of Some Estimators for the Errors-in-Variables Model", The Annals of Statistics 8, 407-422.

Hodges, S.D. and P.G. Moore (1972), "Data Uncertainties and Least Squares Regression", Applied Statistics 21, 185-195.

Jöreskog, K.G. and D. Sörbom (1981), Lisrel V - Analysis of Linear Relationships by Maximum Likelihood and Least Squares Methods, Department of Statistics, University of Uppsala, Uppsala.

Kapteyn, A. and T.J. Wansbeek (1984), Errors in Variables: Consistent Adjusted Least Squares (CALS) Estimation, Communications in Statistics, forthcoming.

Ketellapper, R.H. (1982), "Two-Stage Least Squares Estimation in the Simultaneous Equation Model with Errors in the Variables", The Review of Economics and Statistics 64, 696-701.

Klepper, S. and E.E. Leamer (1984), "Consistent Sets of Estimates for Regressions with Errors in All Variables", Econometrica 52, 163-183.

Leamer, E.E. (1982), "Sets of Posterior Means with Bounded Variance Priors", Econometrica 50, 725-736.

Leamer, E.E. (1983), Destructive Diagnostics for the Errors-in-Variables Model, mimeo, Department of Economics, UCLA, Los Angeles.

Schneeweiss, H. (1976), "Consistent Estimation of a Regression with Errors in the Variables", Metrika 23, 101-115.

Van de Stadt, H., A. Kapteyn and S.A. van de Geer (1983), The Relativity of Utility: Evidence from Panel Data, working paper, Department of Econometrics, Tilburg University, Tilburg.

TESTING PARAMETER CONSTANCY OF LINEAR REGRESSIONS

Herman J. Bierens
Department of Economics
University of Amsterdam
Jodenbreestraat 23
1011 NH Amsterdam

0 ABSTRACT

In this paper we propose a new test for parameter constancy of linear regressions. The alternative hypothesis is that the data set can be split up in a finite number of subsets such that at least two of the OLS estimators corresponding to these subsets have different probability limits. Conditions are set forth such that under the null hypothesis the test statistic involved is asymptotically χ^2 distributed, whereas under the alternative hypothesis the test statistic converges in probability to infinity. These conditions allow for stochastic regressors and time series applications.

1 INTRODUCTION

In regression analysis it is usually assumed that the parameters are the same for all observations. If the data-generating process is heterogeneous, however, this assumption is not obvious. For then the marginal distributions of the observations are not identical, and so could be the conditional expectations corresponding to these marginal distributions. Thus if $\{(y_t, x_t)\}_{t=1}^{\infty}$ is the data-generating process in $\mathbb{R} \times \mathbb{R}^k$ with $\{h_t(y,x)\}_{t=1}^{\infty}$ the sequence of corresponding marginal densities, then

$$E(y_t | x_t = x) = \int_{-\infty}^{+\infty} y h_t(y,x)dy / \int_{-\infty}^{+\infty} h_t(y,x)dy = g_t(x),$$

say, where the regression functions g_t are not necessarily identical if the densities h_t are not identical. On the other hand, heterogeneous data does not automatically rule out invariant regression functions, for it is possible that the conditional expectations $g_t(y|x)$ are identical while the densities $h_t(y,x)$ are not. In the linear regression framework heterogeneity of the regression functions is equivalent with heterogeneity of the parameters, so that we then have

$$y_t = \theta_t' x_t + u_t, \quad t \geqq 1, \tag{1.1}$$

where (u_t) is a sequence of random errors satisfying the standard regression assumption

$$E(u_t | x_t) = 0 \quad \text{(a.s.)}. \tag{1.2}$$

In this paper we propose a test for parameter constancy in linear regressions. Thus the null hypothesis to be tested is:

$$H_0: \; \theta_t = \theta_0 \quad \text{for all} \quad t \geqq 1. \tag{1.3}$$

The ideal alternative hypothesis would be that the null is false. However, this is too a general alternative to be manageable. For example, the case that only a finite number of θ_t's differ from θ_0 can hardly be detected by methods which are only asymptotically valid, as such a case is asymptotically "almost" the same as (1.3). As a second best we therefore consider the class of linear regressions with heterogeneous parameters for which it is possible to split up the data-generating process $\{(y_t,x_t)\}_{t=1}^{\infty}$ into m subprocesses

$$\{(y_{j+(\ell-1)m}, x_{j+(\ell-1)m})\}_{\ell=1}^{\infty} \quad , \quad j = 1,2,\ldots,m,$$

such that at least two of the corresponding OLS statistics

$$\hat{\theta}_{j,n}^{(m)} = \{\tfrac{1}{n}\textstyle\sum_{\ell=1}^{n} x_{j+(\ell-1)m}\, x_{j+(\ell-1)m}'\}^{-1} \tfrac{1}{n}\textstyle\sum_{\ell=1}^{n} x_{j+(\ell-1)m}\, y_{j+(\ell-1)m}, \tag{1.4}$$

$$j = 1,2,\ldots,m,$$

have different probability limits for $n \to \infty$. Thus the alternative hypothesis is:

$$H_1: \text{There exists a possibly unknown integer } m \geq 2 \text{ such that} \tag{1.5}$$
$$\operatorname*{plim}_{n\to\infty} \hat{\theta}^{(m)}_{j_1,n} \neq \operatorname*{plim}_{n\to\infty} \hat{\theta}^{(m)}_{j_2,n} \quad \text{for some } j_1, j_2 \in \{1,\ldots,m\}.$$

The problem of testing the constancy of regression relations has been considered, in different ways, by Chow (1960), Quandt (1960) and Brown, Durbin and Evans (1975), among others. [See for example the whole issue no. 4 of the Annals of Economic and Social Measurement 2 (1973)]. Our approach differs from the literature in that (I) we allow for stochastic regressors which may contain lagged dependent variables, (II) we explicitly deal with the asymptotic power of the test; and (III) we do not assume normality of the disturbances.

Most of the proofs of our results will be given in an extended version of this paper, which is available from the author on request.

2. IDENTIFICATION OF THE NULL HYPOTHESIS VERSUS THE ALTERNATIVE HYPOTHESIS

In this section we show that the hypotheses (1.3) and (1.5) correspond to distinct asymptotic properties of a particular sample function. First, consider the random vector

$$\hat{a}_m = \frac{1}{n}\sum_{t=1}^{n} x_t (y_t - x_t'\hat{\theta}) w_{t,m} \tag{2.1}$$

where $\hat{\theta}$ is the OLS estimator:

$$\hat{\theta} = \left[\frac{1}{n}\sum_{t=1}^{n} x_t x_t'\right]^{-1} \frac{1}{n}\sum_{t=1}^{n} x_t y_t \tag{2.2}$$

and the $w_{t,m}$ are positive weights satisfying

$$w_{j,m} = w_{j+(\ell-1)m,m} \quad \text{for } j = 1,\ldots,m \quad \text{and} \quad \ell \geq 1. \tag{2.3}$$

Moreover, suppose

ASSUMPTION 1 [1]. For $j = 1,\dots,m$,

$$\operatorname*{plim}_{N\to\infty} \frac{1}{N}\sum_{\ell=1}^{N} x_{j+(\ell-1)m}\, x'_{j+(\ell-1)m} = \Omega_{j,m} \quad \text{exists and is positive definite;}$$

$$\operatorname*{plim}_{N\to\infty} \frac{1}{N}\sum_{\ell=1}^{N} x_{j+(\ell-1)m}\, y_{j+(\ell-1)m} = \gamma_{j,m} \quad \text{exists.}$$

Then it can be shown that

$$\operatorname*{plim}_{n\to\infty} \hat{a}_m = \frac{1}{m}\sum_{j=1}^{m} w_{j,m}\, \Omega_{j,m}(\theta^*_{j,m} - \theta^*) = \bar{a}_m \text{ , say,} \tag{2.4}$$

where

$$\theta^*_{j,m} = \Omega^{-1}_{j,m}\, \gamma_{j,m} = \operatorname*{plim}_{n\to\infty} \hat{\theta}^{(m)}_{j,n} \; ; \tag{2.5}$$

$$\theta^* = \Big[\frac{1}{m}\sum_{j=1}^{m} \Omega_{j,m}\Big]^{-1} \frac{1}{m}\sum_{j=1}^{m} \gamma_{j,m} = \operatorname*{plim}_{n\to\infty} \hat{\theta}$$

Furthermore, if

ASSUMPTION 2. For $j = 1,\dots,m$,

$$\operatorname*{plim}_{N\to\infty} \frac{1}{N}\sum_{\ell=1}^{N} x_{j+(\ell-1)m}\, u_{j+(\ell-1)m} = 0,$$

where the u_t's are disturbances satisfying (1.2), then

$$\theta^* = \theta^*_{j,m} = \theta_0 \quad \text{under } H_0 \text{ ,} \tag{2.6}$$

as is not hard to verify, hence

$$\bar{a}_m = 0 \quad \text{under } H_0 . \tag{2.7}$$

On the other hand, if the alternative hypothesis (1.5) is true then $\theta^*_{j,m} - \theta^* \neq 0$ for at least one $j \in \{1,\dots,m\}$, hence, since the $\Omega_{j,m}$ are assumed to be positive definite,

$$\Omega_{j,m}(\theta^*_{j,m} - \theta^*) \neq 0 \quad \text{for some } j \in \{1,\dots,m\} \quad \text{if } H_1 \text{ is true.} \tag{2.8}$$

This implies that we can choose the weights $w_{t,m}$ such that

$$\bar{a}_m \neq 0 \quad \text{under } H_1. \tag{2.9}$$

The question now arises how the weights $w_{j,m}$ should be chosen, as in practice we do not know in advance for which j (2.8) holds if H_1 is true. The answer to this question is suggested by the following easy corollary of Theorem 2 of Bierens (1982).

LEMMA 1. Let $(\alpha_j)_{j=1}^m$ be a sequence of real numbers and let

$$\zeta_m(\tau) = \frac{1}{m}\sum_{j=1}^m \alpha_j \, e^{\tau j/m} .$$

Then $\alpha_j \neq 0$ for some $j \in \{1,\dots,m\}$ if and only if there exists an $\varepsilon > 0$ such that

$$\zeta_m(\tau) \neq 0 \quad \text{for all } \tau \in (0,\varepsilon]. \qquad \square$$

Thus let

$$w_{j,m}(\tau) = e^{\tau(\mathrm{mod}(j-1+m,m)+1)/m} . \tag{2.10}$$

Then (2.3) is satisfied, i.e.

$$w_{j,m}(\tau) = w_{j+(\ell-1)m,m}(\tau) = e^{\tau j/m} \quad \text{for } j = 1,\dots,m \text{ and } \ell \geq 1. \tag{2.11}$$

By changing $w_{j,m}$ in (2.1) to $w_{j,m}(\tau)$ we get

$$\hat{a}_m(\tau) = \frac{1}{n}\sum_{j=1}^n x_j(y_j - x_j'\hat{\theta})w_{j,m}(\tau) \tag{2.12}$$

and (2.4) now becomes

$$\begin{aligned} \operatorname*{plim}_{n\to\infty} \hat{a}_m(\tau) &= \frac{1}{m}\sum_{j=1}^m w_{j,m}(\tau)\Omega_{j,m}(\theta^*_{j,m} - \theta^*) \\ &= \frac{1}{m}\sum_{j=1}^m e^{\tau j/m} \, \Omega_{j,m}(\theta^*_{j,m} - \theta^*) \\ &= \bar{a}_m(\tau) \text{ , say.} \end{aligned} \tag{2.13}$$

Identification of the null hypothesis (1.3) versus the alternative is now provided by the following theorem.

THEOREM 1. Under Assumptions 1 and 2 we have:

(I) $\operatorname*{plim}_{n\to\infty} \sup_{|\tau|\leq K} \| \hat{a}_m(\tau) - \bar{a}_m(\tau) \| = 0$ for every $K\in(0,\infty)$.

(II) If H_0 is true then

$$\bar{a}_m(\tau) = 0 \text{ for all } \tau\in\mathbb{R}$$

(III) If H_1 is true then there exists an $\varepsilon > 0$ such that

$$\bar{a}_m(\tau) \neq 0 \text{ for all } \tau\in(0,\varepsilon].$$ □

3 THE TEST WHEN m IS KNOWN

Theorem 1 suggests to use $\hat{a}_m(\tau)$ for deriving a test statistic, provided m is known under H_1. Indeed, it can be shown that

$$\sqrt{n}\, \hat{a}_m(\tau) \to N_k(0,B_m(\tau)) \quad \text{in distr. under } H_0 \tag{3.1}$$

for every $\tau \in \mathbb{R}$, where $B_m(\tau)$ is, for $\tau \neq 0$, a positive definite covariance matrix. Moreover, part III of Theorem 1 implies that under H_1 there exists an $\varepsilon > 0$ such that

$$\operatorname*{plim}_{n\to\infty} \| \sqrt{n}\, \hat{a}_m(\tau) \| = \infty \quad \text{for all } \tau\in(0,\varepsilon]. \tag{3.2}$$

Furthermore, we shall derive a consistent estimator $\hat{B}_m(\tau)$ of $B_m(\tau)$, thus

$$\operatorname*{plim}_{n\to\infty} \hat{B}_m(\tau) = B_m(\tau) \quad \text{for every } \tau\in \mathbb{R} \text{ if } H_0 \text{ is true} \tag{3.3}$$

which under H_1 also converges in probability, i.e.

$$\operatorname*{plim}_{n\to\infty} \hat{B}_m(\tau) = B_m^*(\tau) \quad \text{for every } \tau\in \mathbb{R} \text{ if } H_1 \text{ is true,} \tag{3.4}$$

where

$$B_m^*(\tau) \text{ is positive definite for } \tau \neq 0. \tag{3.5}$$

These results suggest a test statistic of the form

$$\hat{T}_m(\tau) = n\,\hat{a}_m(\tau)'\,\hat{B}_m(\tau)^{-1}\,\hat{a}_m(\tau), \tag{3.6}$$

for (3.1) and (3.3) imply that

$$\hat{T}_m(\tau) \to \chi_k^2 \text{ in distr. for every } \tau \neq 0 \text{ if } H_0 \text{ is true,} \tag{3.7}$$

whereas (3.2), (3.4) and (3.5) imply that under H_1 there exists an $\varepsilon > 0$ such that

$$\operatorname*{plim}_{n\to\infty} \hat{T}_m(\tau) = \infty \qquad \text{for every } \tau\in(0,\varepsilon]. \tag{3.8}$$

Thus conducting the test at the $\alpha.100\%$ confidence level (with $\alpha\in(0,1)$), we accept H_0 if for an a priori chosen small $\tau_0 > 0$,

$$\hat{T}_m(\tau_0) \leq T(\alpha) \tag{3.9}$$

and we accept H_1 if

$$\hat{T}_m(\tau_0) > T(\alpha), \tag{3.10}$$

where $T(\alpha)$ is such that

$$P(\chi_k^2 \leq T(\alpha)) = 1 - \alpha. \tag{3.11}$$

The power of the test depends, of course, on whether τ_0 is small enough and whether m is correctly specified. Therefore we advocate to conduct the test for various τ_0. Moreover, in Section 4 we shall discuss the case where m is not known in advance.

Denoting

$$\hat{C}_m(\tau) = (\tfrac{1}{n}\textstyle\sum_{t=1}^{n} x_t x_t' w_{t,m}(\tau))(\tfrac{1}{n}\textstyle\sum_{t=1}^{n} x_t x_t')^{-1} , \tag{3.12}$$

the estimator $\hat{B}_m(\tau)$ takes the form

$$\hat{B}_m(\tau) = \tfrac{1}{n}\textstyle\sum_{t=1}^{n} (y_t - \hat{\theta}' x_t)^2 (w_{t,m}(\tau)I - \hat{C}_m(\tau)) x_t x_t' (w_{t,m}(\tau)I - \hat{C}_m(\tau)'). \tag{3.13}$$

The results (3.7) and (3.8) require the following assumptions.

ASSUMPTION 3. For $t \geq 2$, $E(u_t | x_t, x_{t-1}, \ldots, x_1, u_{t-1}, \ldots, u_1) = 0$ a.s. [2]

ASSUMPTION 4. $\sup_{n\geq 1} \frac{1}{n}\sum_{t=1}^{n} E\| u_t x_t \|^{2+\delta} < \infty$ for some $\delta > 0$.

ASSUMPTION 5 [3]. For $j = 1,\ldots,m$,

$$\operatorname*{plim}_{N\to\infty} \tfrac{1}{N}\textstyle\sum_{\ell=1}^{N} (y_{j+(\ell-1)m} - x_{j+(\ell-1)m}'\theta)^2 \, x_{j+(\ell-1)m} \, x_{j+(\ell-1)m}'$$

$$= \lim_{N\to\infty} \tfrac{1}{N}\textstyle\sum_{\ell=1}^{N} E(y_{j+(\ell-1)m} - x_{j+(\ell-1)m}'\theta)^2 \, x_{j+(\ell-1)m} \, x_{j+(\ell-1)m}'$$

$= \Lambda_{j,m}(\theta)$ uniformly on any compact subset of $\mathbb{R}^k$.

ASSUMPTION 6. For $j = 1,\ldots,m$ and $\theta \in \mathbb{R}^k$, $\Lambda_{j,m}(\theta)$ is positive definite.

Summarizing, we now have the following result.

THEOREM 2. Let $\hat{T}_m(\tau)$ be defined by (3.6), with $\hat{B}_m(\tau)$ defined by (3.13). Under Assumptions 1 and 3 through 6 we have

$$\hat{T}_m(\tau) \to \chi_k^2 \quad \text{in distr. for every } \tau \neq 0 \text{ if } H_0 \text{ is true,}$$

whereas, if H_1 is true, there exists an $\varepsilon > 0$ such that

$$\operatorname*{plim}_{n\to\infty} \hat{T}_m(\tau) = \infty \quad \text{for all } \tau \in (0,\varepsilon]. \qquad \square$$

4 THE CASE WHERE m IS UNKNOWN

In the preceding section we have assumed that m is known under H_1. In this section we shall extend our approach to the case where m is only known to be bounded from above by some upperbound $m^* \geq 2$.

Let for $\gamma \in \mathbb{R}$,

$$\hat{a}(\tau,\lambda) = \sum_{m=2}^{m^*} \lambda^{m-2} \hat{a}_m(\tau), \tag{4.1}$$

$$\bar{a}(\tau,\lambda) = \sum_{m=2}^{m^*} \lambda^{m-2} \bar{a}_m(\tau). \tag{4.2}$$

Similarly to Theorem 1 we then have:

THEOREM 3. Under Assumptions 1 and 2,

(I) $\quad \text{plim}_{n\to\infty} \sup_{|\tau|\leq K_1, |\lambda|\leq K_2} |\hat{a}(\tau,\lambda) - \bar{a}(\tau,\lambda)| = 0$

for every $K_1, K_2 \in (0,\infty)$.

(II) If H_0 is true then

$\bar{a}(\tau,\lambda) = 0$ for all $(\tau,\lambda) \in \mathbb{R}^2$.

(III) If H_1 is true then there exists an $\varepsilon > 0$ and for each $\tau \in (0,\varepsilon]$ a $\delta_\tau > 0$ such that

$\bar{a}(\tau,\lambda) \neq 0$ for every $\lambda \in (0,\delta_\tau]$ and $\tau \in (0,\varepsilon]$. □

Moreover, denoting

$$w_j(\tau,\lambda) = \sum_{m=2}^{m^*} \lambda^{m-2} w_{j,m}(\lambda), \tag{4.3}$$

$$\hat{C}(\tau,\lambda) = \sum_{m=2}^{m^*} \lambda^{m-2} \hat{C}_m(\tau) \tag{4.4}$$

$$= \left(\frac{1}{n}\sum_{t=1}^{n} x_t x_t' w_t(\tau,\lambda)\right)\left(\frac{1}{n}\sum_{t=1}^{n} x_t x_t'\right)^{-1},$$

$$\hat{B}(\tau,\lambda) = \tfrac{1}{n}\textstyle\sum_{j=1}^{n}(y_t - \hat{\theta}'x_t)^2(w_t(\tau,\lambda)I - \hat{C}(\tau,\lambda))x_t x_t'(w_t(\tau,\lambda)I - \hat{C}(\tau,\lambda)') \tag{4.5}$$

and

$$\hat{T}(\tau,\lambda) = n\ \hat{a}(\tau,\lambda)'\ \hat{B}(\tau,\lambda)^{-1}\ \hat{a}(\tau,\lambda) \tag{4.6}$$

it follows similarly to Theorem 2 that:

THEOREM 4. Under Assumptions 1 and 3 through 6,

$\hat{T}(\tau,\lambda) \to \chi_k^2$ in distr. for every $\tau \neq 0$ and $\lambda \in \mathbb{R}$ if H_0 is true, whereas, if H_1 is true, there exists an $\varepsilon > 0$ and for each $\tau \in (0,\varepsilon]$ a $\delta_\tau > 0$ such that

$$\operatorname*{plim}_{n\to\infty} \hat{T}(\tau,\lambda) = \infty \quad \text{for all } \lambda \in (0,\delta_\tau] \quad \text{and } \tau \in (0,\varepsilon]. \qquad \square$$

The test may now be conducted in the same way as before. Thus choose a significance level $\alpha \in (0,1)$ and small positive numbers τ_0 and λ_0. Then H_0 is accepted if $\hat{T}(\tau_0,\lambda_0) \leq T(\alpha)$ and H_1 is accepted if $\hat{T}(\tau_0, \lambda_0) > T(\alpha)$, where $T(\alpha)$ is defined by (3.11).

5 SOME NUMERICAL EXAMPLES

In this section we demonstrate the performance of the tests proposed in Sections 3 and 4 by some numerical examples. We have generated 10 data sets $\{(y_1,x_1),\ldots,(y_{100},x_{100})\}$ (thus n=100) according to:

Model 1: $y_t = .5 + .5y_{t-1} + u_t$, $u_t \sim NID(0,1)$,

$x_t = y_{t-1}$,

and we have done the same according to:

Model 2 : $y_t = \alpha_t + \alpha_t y_{t-1} + u_t$, $u_t \sim NID(0,1)$,

$x_t = y_{t-1}$,

where for all integers ℓ:

$$\alpha_{1+(\ell-1)4} = .2$$

$$\alpha_{2+(\ell-1)4} = .4$$

$$\alpha_{3+(\ell-1)4} = .6$$

$$\alpha_{4+(\ell-1)4} = .8$$

For both cases we test the null hypothesis

$$H_0 : y_t = \theta_1 + \theta_2 . x_t + u_t \quad , \quad E(u_t | x_t) = 0 \quad \text{a.s.},$$

where θ_1 and θ_2 do not vary with t. Clearly this null hypothesis is true for model 1 and false for model 2.

Table 1 gives the test results for model 1, where the columns 1 to 10 correspond with each of the 10 artificial data sets involved. Test 1 is the test proposed in Section 3, that is, the figures involved are the values of the test statistic $\hat{T}_m(\tau)$ for m = 4 and τ = .1,.2,.3,.4 and .5, respectively.

Test 2 is the test proposed in Section 4 with test statistic $\hat{T}(\tau,\lambda)$, where τ has the same range as before and also λ goes from .1 to .5. The upperbound m* has been chosen m* = 40. Since in this case the null hypothesis is true, the test statistics $\hat{T}_m(\tau)$ and $\hat{T}(\tau,\lambda)$ are χ_2^2 distributed, hence $P(\hat{T} \geq 5.99) = 0.05$.
Thus if we conduct the test at the 5% significance level then test 1 accepts the true null in all 10 cases and test 2 accepts the true null in 9 out of 10 cases.

The results in Table 2 correspond with model 2. Again conducting the tests at the 5% significance level we see that test 1 rejects the false null in all 10 cases and test 2 rejects the false null in 9 out of 10 cases.

TABLE 1 : HO IS TRUE

TEST 1

m	τ	1	2	3	4	5	6	7	8	9	10
4	0.1	1.50	0.43	0.98	2.50	3.46	0.08	4.52	1.26	0.27	2.18
4	0.2	1.53	0.44	0.98	2.53	3.38	0.09	4.51	1.31	0.28	2.22
4	0.3	1.56	0.45	0.98	2.56	3.30	0.09	4.50	1.36	0.28	2.25
4	0.4	1.59	0.45	0.98	2.59	3.21	0.09	4.49	1.42	0.28	2.29
4	0.5	1.62	0.46	0.98	2.61	3.13	0.10	4.48	1.47	0.29	2.32

TEST 2

τ	λ	1	2	3	4	5	6	7	8	9	10
0.1	0.1	5.68	2.87	5.10	1.01	1.24	1.73	6.95	3.02	0.11	0.55
0.1	0.2	4.95	2.81	5.12	1.11	0.95	1.78	7.19	3.38	0.16	0.47
0.1	0.3	4.22	2.78	5.03	1.23	0.69	1.78	7.36	3.80	0.20	0.42
0.1	0.4	3.55	2.80	4.79	1.37	0.49	1.76	7.48	4.29	0.23	0.38
0.1	0.5	2.99	2.89	4.35	1.54	0.37	1.70	7.53	4.86	0.24	0.32
0.2	0.1	5.70	2.87	5.10	1.01	1.24	1.73	6.94	3.01	0.11	0.55
0.2	0.2	4.98	2.81	5.12	1.11	0.96	1.77	7.18	3.37	0.16	0.48
0.2	0.3	4.26	2.78	5.03	1.22	0.69	1.77	7.35	3.79	0.20	0.43
0.2	0.4	3.59	2.79	4.80	1.37	0.49	1.75	7.46	4.28	0.23	0.39
0.2	0.5	3.03	2.88	4.37	1.54	0.37	1.68	7.51	4.86	0.24	0.33
0.3	0.1	5.71	2.87	5.10	1.01	1.25	1.72	6.94	3.01	0.11	0.56
0.3	0.2	5.00	2.81	5.12	1.11	0.96	1.76	7.17	3.37	0.16	0.48
0.3	0.3	4.29	2.78	5.04	1.22	0.70	1.76	7.33	3.79	0.20	0.44
0.3	0.4	3.63	2.79	4.81	1.36	0.50	1.73	7.44	4.28	0.23	0.40
0.3	0.5	3.08	2.87	4.39	1.53	0.37	1.66	7.49	4.85	0.24	0.34
0.4	0.1	5.72	2.87	5.10	1.01	1.25	1.72	6.93	3.01	0.11	0.56
0.4	0.2	5.03	2.81	5.12	1.11	0.97	1.75	7.16	3.36	0.16	0.49
0.4	0.3	4.33	2.78	5.04	1.22	0.71	1.75	7.32	3.78	0.20	0.44
0.4	0.4	3.67	2.79	4.82	1.36	0.50	1.72	7.42	4.27	0.23	0.41
0.4	0.5	3.12	2.87	4.41	1.53	0.38	1.65	7.47	4.84	0.24	0.35
0.5	0.1	5.73	2.87	5.10	1.01	1.25	1.71	6.93	3.01	0.11	0.56
0.5	0.2	5.05	2.81	5.12	1.10	0.97	1.74	7.15	3.36	0.16	0.49
0.5	0.3	4.36	2.78	5.04	1.21	0.71	1.74	7.30	3.77	0.20	0.45
0.5	0.4	3.71	2.78	4.83	1.36	0.51	1.70	7.40	4.26	0.23	0.41
0.5	0.5	3.16	2.86	4.43	1.53	0.38	1.63	7.44	4.83	0.24	0.36

TABLE 2 : HO IS FALSE

TEST 1

m	τ	1	2	3	4	5	6	7	8	9	10
4	0.1	12.68	20.42	9.82	15.27	25.38	13.23	14.00	21.37	11.17	20.50
4	0.2	12.74	20.37	9.78	15.24	25.28	13.18	13.99	21.32	11.21	20.44
4	0.3	12.79	20.32	9.73	15.21	25.17	13.12	13.98	21.28	11.25	20.39
4	0.4	12.85	20.26	9.69	15.18	25.05	13.06	13.97	21.23	11.29	20.33
4	0.5	12.91	20.20	9.64	15.15	24.94	13.00	13.96	21.18	11.32	20.27

TEST 2

τ	λ	1	2	3	4	5	6	7	8	9	10
0.1	0.1	5.15	9.67	7.85	6.70	9.84	11.23	17.41	13.71	7.62	9.04
0.1	0.2	5.16	10.03	7.53	6.79	9.70	11.04	17.62	13.52	7.80	9.44
0.1	0.3	5.23	10.59	7.26	6.98	9.60	10.75	17.63	13.39	8.09	9.88
0.1	0.4	5.32	11.29	7.11	7.23	9.49	10.41	17.46	13.34	8.40	10.41
0.1	0.5	5.40	12.07	7.13	7.46	9.29	10.10	17.02	13.36	8.60	11.05
0.2	0.1	5.15	9.67	7.86	6.70	9.85	11.23	17.42	13.72	7.62	9.04
0.2	0.2	5.16	10.03	7.55	6.79	9.71	11.05	17.64	13.53	7.80	9.44
0.2	0.3	5.23	10.58	7.29	6.98	9.61	10.75	17.67	13.40	8.09	9.88
0.2	0.4	5.32	11.28	7.14	7.23	9.50	10.42	17.50	13.35	8.41	10.41
0.2	0.5	5.40	12.05	7.16	7.45	9.29	10.09	17.09	13.37	8.62	11.04
0.3	0.1	5.15	9.67	7.87	6.70	9.85	11.24	17.42	13.72	7.62	9.05
0.3	0.2	5.16	10.02	7.57	6.79	9.71	11.06	17.65	13.53	7.80	9.45
0.3	0.3	5.23	10.57	7.32	6.98	9.61	10.76	17.69	13.41	8.09	9.88
0.3	0.4	5.32	11.26	7.18	7.22	9.50	10.42	17.55	13.36	8.42	10.41
0.3	0.5	5.40	12.03	7.19	7.44	9.29	10.08	17.15	13.39	8.64	11.02
0.4	0.1	5.15	9.67	7.88	6.70	9.85	11.24	17.43	13.72	7.62	9.05
0.4	0.2	5.16	10.02	7.60	6.79	9.72	11.07	17.67	13.54	7.80	9.45
0.4	0.3	5.23	10.56	7.36	6.97	9.62	10.77	17.72	13.42	8.10	9.88
0.4	0.4	5.32	11.24	7.21	7.21	9.50	10.42	17.59	13.37	8.43	10.40
0.4	0.5	5.40	12.01	7.22	7.43	9.30	10.08	17.21	13.40	8.66	11.01
0.5	0.1	5.15	9.67	7.89	6.70	9.85	11.25	17.44	13.72	7.62	9.05
0.5	0.2	5.16	10.02	7.62	6.79	9.72	11.08	17.68	13.54	7.80	9.45
0.5	0.3	5.23	10.55	7.39	6.97	9.62	10.78	17.75	13.42	8.10	9.89
0.5	0.4	5.32	11.23	7.25	7.20	9.51	10.43	17.63	13.38	8.43	10.40
0.5	0.5	5.40	11.99	7.25	7.42	9.30	10.07	17.26	13.41	8.67	10.99

In view of the small sample size of 100, the above results are satisfactory. Of course, definite conclusions about the general performance of our tests can not be drawn from these results. The purpose of these numerical examples, however, is merely to show that our approach might have practical significance. Obviously the above results provide evidence for that.

Notes

1) This assumption can be derived from further conditions, using Lemma 3 of Bierens (1984). These further conditions allow the data-generating process to be a dependent vector time series process.

2) This assumption implies that model (1.1) represents the conditional expectation of y_t given x_t and the past of $\{(y_t,x_t)\}$, i.e.

   $x_t'\theta_t = E(y_t|x_t,x_{t-1},\ldots,x_1,y_{t-1},\ldots,y_1)$ a.s. for $t \geq 2$.

3) This assumption can be derived from further conditions, using Lemma 3 of Bierens (1984).

REFERENCES

Bierens, H.J., 1982, "Consistent Model Specifications Tests", Journal of Econometrics 20, 105-134.

Bierens, H.J., 1984, "Model Specification Testing of Time Series Regressions", Journal of Econometrics 27 (forthcoming).

Brown, R.L., J. Durbin and J.M. Evans, 1975, "Techniques for Testing the Constancy of Regression Relationships over Time" (with discussion), Journal of the Royal Statistical Society, Series B 37, 149-192.

Quandt, R.E., 1960, "Tests of the Hypothesis that a Linear Regression System Obeys Two Separate Regimes", Journal of the American Statistical Association 55, 324-330.

PREDICTION PERFORMANCE AND THE NUMBER OF VARIABLES IN MULTIVARIATE LINEAR REGRESSION

Ton Steerneman
Econometrics Institute
University of Groningen
P.O. Box 800, 9700 AV Groningen
The Netherlands

0. ABSTRACT

The multivariate linear regression model is considered for prediction purposes. It will be assumed that there are in principle infinitely many regressors ordered according to decreasing importance. The conditional variance of the regressand given the first p regressors will be denoted by ω_p^2. A natural measure of the performance of regression-predictors is mean squared prediction error MSEP(n,p), n being the sample size and p the number of variables. If $\{\omega_p^2\}$ is known, then p will be chosen such that MSEP(n,p) is minimized. Typically, this may give an optimal p* much smaller than n; in other words it pays to delete variables when coefficients have to be estimated. In practice the quantity MSEP(n,p) is unknown but it can be unbiasedly estimated by msep(n,p), the so-called S_p-criterion. It is frequently suggested to choose the number of variables $\hat{p}$ such that msep(n,p) is minimized. This rule is asymptotically optimal in the sense that msep$(n,\hat{p})$/MSEP(n,p*) $\to$ 1 in probability as $n \to \infty$. It will be shown that there are a lot of other selection-of-variables procedures, which share this property. So, asymptotic optimality is by itself not very compelling, and minimization of the S_p-criterion needs more justification.

1. INTRODUCTION

The advance of computer technology led to a revolutionary growth of the use of statistical methodology in various disciplines. Important features of the computer are

(i) automatic data recording and handling,

(ii) the possibility to store and retrieve an enormous amount of data,

(iii) high computation speed.

With regard to statistical applications it is possible to study the implications of various alternative models, included those leading to heavy computations. Thanks to the computer we can now evaluate much larger models than in the old days when calculations had to be done by hand. However, the sample sizes are quite often not large compared with the number of observable variables. One can always think of more characteristics to measure. So, with the computational burden largely removed, there is a real temptation to build models with large numbers of variables. The danger inherent to such a use of the computer is not realizing that statistical procedures may suffer from a so-called peaking phenomenon: they may show a decreasing actual performance if the number of variables is increased beyond a certain bound. Although the problem was recognized many decades ago, presently it is really actual. It frequently happens that a set of variables is chosen which performs best in the sample without realizing that this performance is data-dependent and hence uncertain. The data are used twice, first for selecting the variables, and secondly the model is analyzed as if the variables were predetermined. At this second step the uncertainties involved in the choice of the variables are not taken into account. So the improvement in performance obtained may be quite illusory. For some literature regarding the subject we refer to e.g. Hocking (1976), Thompson (1978), Judge and Bock (1978), Stone (1981), Lovell (1983), Breiman and Freedman (1983), Freedman (1983), Krishnaiah and Kanal, eds. (1983), and the references in each of these publications.

In section 2 we shall introduce the multivariate linear regression model, and we describe the aims which may be of interest. We will focus on the aim of prediction. A natural performance measure is the mean squared prediction error (MSEP). In section 3 the MSEP's for classical predictors will be studied, especially their asymptotic behaviour as the sample size tends to infinity. In section 4 the S_p-criterion, which is used in practice for selecting the variables, will be evaluated. In this article proofs will not be given, the interested reader is referred to Steerneman (1984).

2. THE MULTIVARIATE LINEAR REGRESSION MODEL

Let the random variables $Y, X_1, X_2, \ldots$ be jointly normally distributed. Define $\underline{X} = (X_1, X_2, \ldots)^t$ and let $\underline{Z} = (Y, \underline{X}^t)^t$. We write

$$\underline{Z} \sim N_\infty(\eta, \Omega), \tag{2.1}$$

where η and Ω are partitioned as follows

$$\eta = \begin{pmatrix} \mu \\ \nu \end{pmatrix} \text{ and } \Omega = \begin{pmatrix} \omega_0^2 & \Omega_o^t \\ \Omega_0 & \Sigma \end{pmatrix}$$

with μ, $\omega_0 \in \mathbb{R}$. We write

$$\nu = (\nu_1, \nu_2, \ldots)^t, \ \Omega_0 = (\omega_{01}, \omega_{02}, \ldots)^t \text{ and } \Sigma = (\sigma_{ij}).$$

Let $\underline{X}^{(p)} = (X_1, \ldots, X_p)^t$, $\underline{Z}^{(p)} = (Y, X_1, \ldots, X_p)^t$, $\nu^{(p)} = (\nu_1, \ldots, \nu_p)^t$, $\eta^{(p)} = (\mu, \nu_1, \ldots$ $\ldots, \nu_p)^t$, $\Omega_0^{(p)} = (\omega_{01}, \ldots, \omega_{0p})^t$, $\Sigma^{(p)} = (\sigma_{ij})_{i,j=1,\ldots,p}$ and

$$\Omega^{(p)} = \begin{pmatrix} \omega_0^2 & \Omega_0^{(p)^t} \\ \Omega_0^{(p)} & \Sigma^{(p)} \end{pmatrix}.$$

We have

$$\underline{Z}^{(p)} \sim N_{p+1}(\eta^{(p)}, \Omega^{(p)}). \tag{2.2}$$

For p = 0 we define $\underline{Z}^{(0)} = Y$, $\eta^{(0)} = \mu$, $\Omega^{(0)} = \omega_0^2$. It will be assumed that $\Omega^{(p)}$ is nonsingular for p = 0,1,2,... . From (2.1) or (2.2) it follows that

$$\mathcal{L}(Y|\underline{X}^{(p)}) = N(\mu+\Omega_0^{(p)^t}\Sigma^{(p)^{-1}}(\underline{X}^{(p)}-\nu^{(p)}), \omega_p^2), \tag{2.3}$$

where

$$\omega_p^2 = \omega_0^2 - \Omega_0^{(p)^t}\Sigma^{(p)^{-1}}\Omega_0^{(p)}. \tag{2.4}$$

According to (2.3) we have the linear regression

$$Y = \alpha(p) + \underline{X}^{(p)^t}\beta(p) + \varepsilon(p), \tag{2.5}$$

where

$$\beta(p) = \Sigma^{(p)^{-1}}\Omega_0^{(p)}, \quad \alpha(p) = \mu - \nu^{(p)^t}\beta(p),$$

$$\varepsilon(p) \sim N(0,\omega_p^2),$$

$\underline{X}^{(p)}$ and $\varepsilon^{(p)}$ are independently distributed.

Let us define $Y^*(p)$ by

$$Y = Y^*(p) + \varepsilon(p). \tag{2.6}$$

Hence

$$Y^*(p) = \underline{X}^{(p)^t}\beta(p) + \alpha(p) \sim N(\mu,\omega_0^2-\omega_p^2).$$

For p = 0 we define, of course, $Y^*(0) = \mu$. From (2.6) we see that for any p the regressand can be split up into a systematic part and a disturbance.

It will be assumed that the variables are ordered in such a way that 'those variables come first, which are expected to be more important'. The analysis would be hopelessly complicated without this assumption. If we restrict the attention to a finite number of variables, say p, then these will be the first p ones, and the usual multivariate linear regression model occurs. It is natural to inquire what happens when $p \to \infty$. The answer is given by the following result.

THEOREM 2.1. The sequence $\{Y^*(p)\}$ converges to a limit $Y^*(\infty)$ almost surely and in L_1, and

$$\mathcal{L}Y^*(\infty) = N(\mu,\omega_0^2-\omega_\infty^2), \text{ where } \omega_\infty^2 = \lim_{p\to\infty}\omega_p^2.$$

So we can write $Y = Y^*(\infty) + \varepsilon(\infty)$, where $Y^*(\infty)$ and $\varepsilon(\infty)$ are independently distributed and $\varepsilon(\infty) \sim N(0,\omega_\infty^2)$. Breiman and Freedman (1983) assume that $\omega_\infty^2 > 0$. In other words, they assume that it is not possible to give a complete description of Y in terms of $X_1, X_2, \ldots$. We will deal with $\omega_\infty^2 > 0$ as well as with $\omega_\infty^2 = 0$.

In practice the parameters η and Ω are unknown. We assume that we have at our disposal an independent sample $\underline{Z}_1,\ldots,\underline{Z}_n$ with $\mathcal{L}\underline{Z}_i = \mathcal{L}\underline{Z}$ for $i=1,\ldots,n$ $(n \geqq 3)$. In fact we are interested in $\underline{Z}_1^{(p)},\ldots,\underline{Z}_n^{(p)}$ for $p < n-2$. In such multivariate regression situations several aims may be of interest:

AIM 1. To test whether Y and $\underline{X}$ are independent.

AIM 2. To select a subset of the components of $\underline{X}$ mainly for the purpose of future work reduction.

AIM 3. To estimate the parameters $\alpha(p)$, $\beta(p)$ or ω_p^2, possibly with a confidence interval.

AIM 4. To construct a procedure for predicting Y, possibly with a prediction interval.

It is important to formulate the aim of the research, because the selection of the variables depends on the criterion used which on its turn is determined by the objective of the research-worker, see also Amemiya (1980).

Our aim will be to predict Y_0 on the basis of a realization of $\underline{X}_0$, where $\mathcal{L}\underline{Z}_0 = \mathcal{L}\underline{Z}$ and $\underline{Z}_0$ is independently distributed of $\underline{Z}_1,\ldots,\underline{Z}_n$.

If $\hat{Y}_0$ is a predictor of Y_0, then a natural measure of its performance is the mean squared prediction error

$$\text{MSEP}(\hat{Y}_0) = E(Y_0-\hat{Y}_0)^2.$$

We shall consider classical predictors only.

The relevant statistics are $\overline{\underline{Z}}$, $\underline{T}$ and $\underline{X}_0$, where

$$\overline{\underline{Z}} = n^{-1}\sum_{i=1}^{n}\underline{Z}_i,$$

$$T = \sum_{i=1}^{n}(\underline{Z}_i-\overline{\underline{Z}})(\underline{Z}_i-\overline{\underline{Z}})^t.$$

It is well-known that $(\overline{\underline{Z}}^{(p)},\underline{T}^{(p)})$ is complete sufficient for $(\eta^{(p)},\Omega^{(p)})$, and that

$$\overline{\underline{Z}}^{(p)} \sim N_{p+1}(\eta^{(p)},n^{-1}\Omega^{(p)}),$$

$$\underline{T}^{(p)} \sim W_{p+1}(n-1,\Omega^{(p)}),$$

$\overline{\underline{Z}}^{(p)}$ and $T^{(p)}$ are independently distributed.

We will partition $\underline{\bar{Z}}$ and $\underline{T}$ as follows

$$\underline{\bar{Z}} = \begin{pmatrix} \bar{Y} \\ \underline{\bar{X}} \end{pmatrix} \text{ and } \underline{T} = \begin{pmatrix} t_0^2 & \underline{T}_0^t \\ \underline{T}_0 & \underline{S} \end{pmatrix}.$$

The classical predictor of Y_0 is

$$\hat{Y}_0^{(p)} = a(p) + \underline{X}_0^{(p)^t} \underline{b}(p),$$

where

$$\underline{b}(p) = \underline{S}^{(p)^{-1}} \underline{T}_0^{(p)},$$
$$a(p) = \bar{Y} - \underline{\bar{X}}^{(p)^t} \underline{b}(p).$$

The performance of $\hat{Y}_0^{(p)}$ is

$$\text{MSEP}(n,p) = \text{MSEP}(\hat{Y}_0^{(p)}) = n^{-1}(n+1)(n-2)(n-p-2)^{-1}\omega_p^2. \tag{2.7}$$

If $p = 0$, then Y_0 is predicted by $\bar{Y}$. Formula (2.7) is well-known, but it is not easy to derive. It results from Stein (1960), formulas (2.10), (2.11) and (2.23). A similar proof is also given by Oliker (1978). Steerneman (1984) presents another method. Breiman and Freedman (1983) derive the MSEP for $\eta = 0$.

3. THE BEHAVIOUR OF MSEP

In the classical framework Y_0 would be predicted with $\hat{Y}_0(k)$ on the basis of the variables $X_1,\ldots,X_k$ ($k < n-2$), and this set of variables would essentially be considered as fixed. Intuitively one might think that the quality of the predictor, based on a subset of these k variables, is less than the quality attainable by using the full set, because in the latter case the predictor is based on less information. However, the more variables are introduced in the analysis the more uncertainties are involved. So it may be worthwhile to compare predictors based on different subsets of variables. Since we assumed that the variables are ordered, the only subsets of interest are $\phi,\{X_1\},\{X_1,X_2\},\ldots,\{X_1,\ldots,X_k\}$. The number k denotes the maximum number of variables which can be taken into account. In order to avoid deterioration we will assume that $k < n-2$. In practical situations we often have $k < \frac{1}{2}n$.

Observe that MSEP(n,p) as given in formula (2.7) does not depend on the parameter η, and depends on Ω only through ω_p^2. Note that $\{\omega_p^2\}$ is decreasing and that $(n-p-2)^{-1}$ is increasing in p. Consequently MSEP(n,p) as a function of $p \in \{0,\ldots,k\}$ is minimized by p^*, say, which is possibly quite smaller than k. In other words, the gain obtained by adding variables may be outweighed by an increased uncertainty regarding the coefficients. We will always take p^* as small as possible, when there are more solutions. The classical prediction procedure may show a peaking phenomenon: it may happen that the performance increases if variables are added up to and including p*, and decreases if more variables are introduced. In fact the peaking effect is a sample phenomenon.

In this section we will study the asymptotic behaviour of MSEP(n,p(n)) for sequences $\{p(n)\}$ with $p(n) \in \{0,\ldots,k(n)\}$. The maximum number of variables k will also depend on the sample size. The sequence $\{p^*(n)\}$ deserves special attention.

The following theorem collects some statements easily derived from (2.7). Roughly speaking, if we allow the number of variables to grow in a rate negligible compared to n we will eventually be able to predict the systematic part of Y_0 perfectly.

THEOREM 3.1. Let $k(n)\to\infty$. Let $\{p(n)\}$ be a sequence with $p(n) \in \{0,\ldots,k(n)\}$. If $p(n) \to \infty$ and $p(n)/n \to 0$, then $MSEP(n,p(n)) \to \omega_\infty^2$. Conversely, if $MSEP(n,p(n)) \to \omega_\infty^2$ then $p(n) \to \infty$, and if additionally $\omega_\infty^2 > 0$ then $p(n)/n \to 0$.

COROLLARY 3.2. Let $k(n) \to \infty$, then $p^*(n)\to\infty$ and $MSEP(n,p^*(n)) \to \omega_\infty^2$. If $\omega_\infty^2 > 0$, then $p^*(n)/n \to 0$.

Concerning the second part of corollary 3.2 reference has to be made to Breiman and Freedman (1983).

The next theorem gives some finite sample properties of p*(n), the most economical number of variables. Part of this theorem uses the assumption that $\{\omega_{p+1}^2/\omega_p^2\}$ is nondecreasing. To interpret this assumption it is useful to note that the quantity $\{(\omega_p^2-\omega_{p+1}^2)/\omega_p^2\}^{\frac{1}{2}}$ is equal to the conditional correlation of Y and X_{p+1} given $X_1,\ldots,X_p$. Consequently, a nondecreasing $\{\omega_{p+1}^2/\omega_p^2\}$ implies that the variables are ordered according to non-increasing conditional correlation coefficients.

THEOREM 3.2.

(i) If $k(n) \leqq k(n+1)$, then $p^*(n) \leqq p^*(n+1)$.

(ii) If $\{\omega_{p+1}^2/\omega_p^2\}$ is nondecreasing, then MSEP(n,p) is unimodal on $\{0,\ldots,k(n)\}$, i.e. MSEP(n,p) is decreasing on $\{0,\ldots,p^*\}$ and increasing on $\{p^*+1,\ldots,k(n)\}$.

(iii) If $k(n) \leqq k(n+1)$, $\{\omega_{p+1}^2/\omega_p^2\}$ is nondecreasing and if $k(n+1) \leqq k(n)+1$ or $p^*(n) < k(n)$, then $p^*(n) \leqq p^*(n+1) \leqq p^*(n)+1$.

In case (iii) of theorem 3.2 we see that one new observation does not lead to a drastical change in the optimum number p*(n): the new optimum number p*(n+1) equals the old one or one extra variable should be added.

The following theorem presents some large sample properties of p*(n) in case that $k(n) = n-3$ and $\{\omega_{p+1}^2/\omega_p^2\}$ is nondecreasing. The asymptotical behaviour of p*(n) can easily be derived from the asymptotical behaviour of $\{\omega_p^2\}$.

THEOREM 3.3. Let $k(n) = n-3$ and let $\{\omega_{p+1}^2/\omega_p^2\}$ be nondecreasing, then $\omega_{p+1}^2/\omega_p^2 \to 1$ if and only if $n-p^*(n) \to \infty$.
If $\omega_{p+1}^2/\omega_p^2 \to 1$ then $\delta \in [0,\infty]$ is a limit point of $\{p(1-\omega_{p+1}^2/\omega_p^2)\}$ if and only if $\delta/(1+\delta)$ is a limit point of $\{p^*/n\}$.

4. EVALUATION OF THE S_p CRITERION

In practice, of course, we do not know p^*, because it depends on the unknown parameters $\{\omega_p^2\}$. It has been proposed (see e.g. Hocking (1976) and Thompson (1978)) to replace ω_p^2 by its UMVU estimator

$$\hat{\omega}_p^2 = (n-p-1)^{-1}(t_0^2 - T_0^{(p)^t} S^{(p)^{-1}} T_0^{(p)}),$$

and to estimate p^* by $\hat{p}$ obtained by minimizing the S_p criterion

$$\mathrm{msep}(n,p) = n^{-1}(n+1)(n-2)(n-p-2)^{-1}\hat{\omega}_p^2,$$

and taking the least possible solution. For $p = 0$ we define $\hat{\omega}_p^2 = (n-1)^{-1}t_0^2$. Note that MSEP denotes the actual performance and msep its UMVU estimator as defined above. When $\hat{p}$ has been determined Y_0 it predicted by $\hat{Y}_{0\hat{p}}$.

It seems to be interesting to study the distribution of

$$\mathrm{msep}(n) = \mathrm{msep}(n,0),\ldots,\mathrm{msep}(n,k(n)))^t$$

as an estimator of

$$\mathrm{MSEP}(n) = (\mathrm{MSEP}(n,0),\ldots,\mathrm{MSEP}(n,k(n)))^t.$$

We define

$$U_p = (n-p-1)\hat{\omega}_p^2, \qquad p = 0,\ldots,k(n)$$

and so we can write

$$\mathrm{msep}(n,p) = n^{-1}(n+1)(n-2)(n-p-1)^{-1}(n-p-2)^{-1}U_p.$$

The joint distribution of $U_0,\ldots,U_{k(n)}$ is given by the following result.

THEOREM 4.1. Define $\Delta U_p = U_p - U_{p+1}$, $p = 0,\ldots,k(n)-1$, then

(i) $\Delta U_0, \Delta U_1, \ldots, \Delta U_{k(n)-1}$ and $U_{k(n)}$ are independently distributed,

(ii) $\Delta U_p \sim \omega_{p+1}^2 G\chi'^2(1;\tfrac{1}{2}(n-p-1), 2(\omega_p^2\omega_{p+1}^{-2}-1))$ and $U_{k(n)} \sim \omega_{k(n)}^2 \chi_{n-k(n)-1}^2$.

The gammaized noncentral χ^2 distribution is defined as follows: let $A|B \sim \chi'^2_{d;B}$ and $B \sim G(\alpha,\beta)$, then $A \sim G\chi'^2(d;\alpha,\beta)$.

From theorem 4.1 we observe that the distribution of msep(n) depends on the unknown parameters only through $\{\omega_p^2\}$. However $\mathcal{L}$msep(n) is extremely complicated and therefore normal approximations may be of interest. Note that the vector of msep's has a growing number of components as $k(n) \to \infty$. So, the usual concepts of weak convergence do not apply. For that reason we use the stronger concept of total variation convergence (see the appendix). The proof of the following theorem uses the concept of Hellinger affinity.

THEOREM 4.2. For some $\varepsilon > 0$ let

(i) $\liminf_{p \to \infty} p^{\varepsilon}(1-\omega_{p+1}^2/\omega_p^2) > 0$,

(ii) $[k(n)]^{\varepsilon+1}/n \to 0$,

then

$$\|\mathcal{L}\text{msep}(n)-N_{k(n)+1}(\text{MSEP}(n),\text{VAR}(\text{msep}(n)))\| \to 0$$

as $n \to \infty$, where for $0 \leqq i \leqq j \leqq k(n)$

$$\text{cov}(\text{msep}(n,i),\text{msep}(n,j)) = 2(n-j-2)(n-i-1)^{-1}(n-i-2)^{-1}\{\text{MSEP}(n,j)\}^2.$$

Having this result we would like to apply it in order to study the asymptotic behaviour of msep$(n,\hat{p}(n))$. We have to check the conditions. Assume that $\{\omega_{p+1}^2/\omega_p^2\}$ is nondecreasing and $\varepsilon \leqq 1$. According to theorem 3.3 we have in case $k(n) = n-3$ that $\liminf p^*(n)/n > 0$. Theorem 4.2 requires that $[k(n)]^{\varepsilon+1}/n \to 0$. Hence for n large enough we have $p^*(n) = k(n)$ on account of theorem 3.2(ii). In this situation it would be better to enlarge k(n), when this is possible, and a larger p* wil be achieved leading to a smaller MSEP. For our purposes the conditions of the theorem are too restrictive, when $\varepsilon \leqq 1$, and hence we have to find another way to study msep$(n,\hat{p}(n))$.

Breiman and Freedman (1983) take $k = \frac{1}{2}n$. For the moment we shall assume that $n - k(n) \to \infty$, which is a weaker requirement. A key result is

THEOREM 4.3. Let $n - k(n) \to \infty$, then

$$\max_{p=0}^{k(n)} \|\mathcal{L}(\text{msep}(n,p)/\text{MSEP}(n,p)) - N(1,2(n-p-1)^{-1})\| \to 0.$$

COROLLARY 4.4. If $n - k(n) \to \infty$, then for any sequence $\{p(n)\}$ with $p(n) \in \{0,\dots,k(n)\}$ it holds

$$\text{msep}(n,p(n))/\text{MSEP}(n,p(n)) \overset{P}{\to} 1.$$

The result of the corollary can be strenghtened in a number of cases.

THEOREM 4.5. Let $\omega_\infty^2 > 0$ and $n - k(n) \to \infty$. Let $p(n)$ be a sequence with $p(n) \in \{0,\dots,k(n)\}$. If $p(n)n^{-\frac{1}{2}} \to \infty$ or $n^{\frac{1}{2}}(\omega_{p(n)}^2 - \omega_\infty^2) \to \infty$, then

$$[\text{msep}(n,p(n)) - \omega_\infty^2]/[\text{MSEP}(n,p(n)) - \omega_\infty^2] \xrightarrow{P} 1. \tag{4.1}$$

A selection-of-variables rule can be considered as a random variable $Q(n)$ with values in $\{0,\dots,k(n)\}$. The outcome of $Q(n)$ will depend on the realization of $\underline{Z}_1,\dots,\underline{Z}_n$ and $\underline{X}_0$. If we use the S_p criterion then we have $Q(n) = \hat{p}(n)$. We say that $\{Q_n\}$ is asymptotically optimal if

$$\text{msep}(n,Q(n))/\text{MSEP}(n,p^*(n)) \xrightarrow{P} 1.$$

THEOREM 4.6. Let $n - k(n) \to \infty$, then $\{\hat{p}(n)\}$ is asymptotically optimal.

The S_p criterion is asymptotically optimal. However, there are a lot of other procedures which possess this property. Theorems 4.7-8 can be applied to establish asymptotic optimality of selection-of-variables procedures.

THEOREM 4.7. Let $n - k(n) \to \infty$ and $\omega_\infty^2 > 0$. If $\{Q(n)\}$ is any sequence of random variables with $Q(n) \in \{0,\dots,k(n)\}$, then $Q(n) \xrightarrow{P} \infty$ and $Q(n)/n \xrightarrow{P} 0$ if and only if $\text{msep}(n,Q(n))/\text{MSEP}(n,p^*(n)) \xrightarrow{P} 1$.

In case $\omega_\infty^2 = 0$ things are more complicated, but we can derive a similar result.

THEOREM 4.8. Let $k(n) = n-3$, $\{\omega_{p+1}^2/\omega_p^2\}$ be a nondecreasing sequence, $\omega_\infty^2 = 0$, $\limsup_{p\to\infty} p(1-\omega_{p+1}^2/\omega_p^2) < \infty$ and let $\{Q(n)\}$ be a sequence of random variables with $Q(n) \in \{0,\dots,k(n)\}$ and $n^{-1}(Q(n)-p^*(n)) \xrightarrow{P} 0$. If one of the following conditions is satisfied

(i) $p^*(n)/n \to 0$ and $Q(n)/p^*(n) > M^{-1}$ for some $M > 1$,

(ii) $\liminf_{n\to\infty} p^*(n)/n > 0$,

then

$$\text{msep}(n,Q(n))/\text{MSEP}(n,p^*(n)) \xrightarrow{P} 1.$$

We conclude that the S_p criterion is 'asymptotically optimal', but there are a lot of other variable selection procedures which possess the same asymptotic properties. Hence asymptotic optimality is by itself not a compelling property of the S_p criterion, and it cannot be considered as a straight recommendation to use it in practice. For instance, let $k(n) = \frac{1}{2}n$ and $\omega_\infty^2 > 0$, then the simple choice $Q(n) = \log n$ is 'asymptotically optimal'.

ACKNOWLEDGEMENTS. The author would like to thank Dr. T.K. Dijkstra, Dr. A.E. Ronner and Prof.Dr. W. Schaafsma for stimulating discussions.

APPENDIX. SOMETHING ABOUT TOTAL VARIATION NORM AND HELLINGER AFFINITY

In this appendix $(\mathfrak{X},\mathfrak{F})$ will denote a measurable space. If λ is a finite signed measure on $(\mathfrak{X},\mathfrak{F})$, then $|\lambda|$ will denote the total variation of λ. The total variation norm of λ is $\|\lambda\| = |\lambda|(\mathfrak{X})$. The set of probability measures on $(\mathfrak{X},\mathfrak{F})$ will be denoted by $\mathfrak{M}_1(\mathfrak{X},\mathfrak{F})$. It becomes a metric space by endowing it with the so-called total variation metric defined by

$$d_{tv}(P,Q) = \|P-Q\| \qquad \forall P,Q \in \mathfrak{M}_1(\mathfrak{X},\mathfrak{F}).$$

Note that $0 \leqq d_{tv} \leqq 2$.

If P and Q are probability measures on $(\mathfrak{X},\mathfrak{F})$ then a σ-finite measure λ on $(\mathfrak{X},\mathfrak{F})$ exists such that $P,Q \ll \lambda$ (e.g. $\lambda = P+Q$). If λ is a σ-finite measure, then $P,Q \ll \lambda$ is equivalent with $P+Q \ll \lambda$. There exist $\mathfrak{F}$-measurable functions $p,q\colon \mathfrak{X} \to [0,\infty)$ such that p and q are versions of the Radon-Nikodym derivatives of P and Q with respect to λ; we say that p and q are density functions of P and Q with respect to λ.

PROPOSITION A.1. Let $P,Q \in \mathfrak{M}_1(\mathfrak{X},\mathfrak{F})$, then

$$d_{tv}(P,Q) = 2\sup_{B\in\mathfrak{F}} |P(B)-Q(B)| = \int_{\mathfrak{X}} |p-q|\,d\lambda.$$

Another distance concept is based on the Hellinger affinity

$$\rho(P,Q) = \int_{\mathfrak{X}} p^{\frac{1}{2}}q^{\frac{1}{2}}\,d\lambda.$$

This quantity does not depend on the choice of λ. From the Cauchy-Schwartz inequality it follows that $0 \leqq \rho \leqq 1$.
The Hellinger metric between P and Q is defined by

$$d_H(P,Q) = \{2-2\rho(P,Q)\}^{\frac{1}{2}} = \{\int_{\mathfrak{X}} (p^{\frac{1}{2}}-q^{\frac{1}{2}})^2 d\lambda\}^{\frac{1}{2}}.$$

Note that $0 \leqq d_H \leqq 2^{\frac{1}{2}}$.
The total variation and Hellinger metric are invariant under reduction by sufficiency.

PROPOSITION A.2. Let $(\mathfrak{X},\mathfrak{F})$ and $(\mathcal{Y},\mathcal{G})$ be measurable spaces and $T\colon \mathfrak{X} \to \mathcal{Y}$ a measurable transformation, then

$$d_{tv}(P\circ T^{-1},Q\circ T^{-1}) \leqq d_{tv}(P,Q)$$

and

$$d_H(P\circ T^{-1},Q\circ T^{-1}) \leqq d_H(P,Q).$$

The equality sign holds if T is sufficient statistic for the experiment $(\mathcal{X},\mathcal{F},\{P,Q\})$.

The total variation and Hellinger metric generate the same uniformity structure and thus the same topology on $\mathcal{M}_1(\mathcal{X},\mathcal{F})$.

PROPOSITION A.3 (Kraft). For any $P,Q \in \mathcal{M}_1(\mathcal{X},\mathcal{F})$

$$d_H^2(P,Q) \leqq d_{tv}(P,Q) \leqq 2(1-\rho^2(P,Q))^{\frac{1}{2}} \leqq 2d_H(P,Q).$$

Regarding the total variation and Hellinger metric we refer to Kraft (1955), Lecam (1973), Steerneman (1982) and (1983), and Yosida (1978), sections XII.2-3.

The reason for introducing the Hellinger metric is that it is in practice more easy to handle then the total variation metric.

REFERENCES

Amemiya, T. (1980), Selection of regressors; International Economic Review, vol. 21, 331-354.

Breiman, L. and D. Freedman (1983), How many variables should be entered in a regression equation?; Journal of the American Statistical Association, vol. 78, 131-136.

Freedman, D.A. (1983), A note on screening regression equations; The American Statistician, vol. 37, 152-155.

Hocking, R.R. (1976), The analysis and selection of variables in linear regression; Biometrics, vol. 32, 1-49.

Judge, G.G. and M.E. Bock (1978), The statistical implications of pre-test and Stein-rule estimators in Econometrics; North-Holland, Amsterdam, New York, Oxford.

Kraft, C.H. (1955), Some conditions for consistency and uniform consistency of statistical procedures; University of California Publications in Statistics, vol. 2, 125-141.

Krishnaiah, P.R. and L.N. Kanal, editors (1983), Handbook of Statistics, vol. 2; Classification, Pattern Recognition and Reduction of Dimensionality, North-Holland, Amsterdam, New York, Oxford.

LeCam, L. (1973), Convergence of estimates under dimensionality restrictions; The Annals of Statistics, vol. 1, 38-53.

Lovell, M.C. (1978), Data mining; The review of Economics and Statistics, vol. 65, 1-12.

Oliker, V.I. (1978), On the relationship between the sample size and the number of variables in a linear regression model; Communications in Statistics, Theory and Methods, vol. A7, 509-516.

Steerneman, A.G.M. (1982), Total variation and Hellinger metric on a space of probability measures; the affinity function; Report TW-241, Mathematics Institute, University of Groningen.

Steerneman, A.G.M. (1983), On the total variation and Hellinger distance between signed measures; an application to product measures; Proceedings of the American Mathematical Society, vol. 88, 684-688.

Steerneman, A.G.M. (1984), Prediction performance and the number of variables in multivariate linear regression; theorems and proofs; Report 84-01-SE, Econometrics Institute, University of Groningen.

Stein, Ch. (1960), Multiple regression; ch. 37 of Contributions to Probability and Statistics (Essays in Honor of Harold Hotelling), edited by I. Olkin, S.G. Ghurye, W. Hoeffding, W.G. Madow, H.B. Mann; Stanford University Press, Stanford California.

Stone, Ch.J. (1981), Admissable selection of an accurate and parsimonious normal linear regression model; The Annals of Statistics, vol. 9, 475-485.

Thompson, M.L. (1978), Selection of variables in multiple regression; International Statistical Review, vol. 46, 1-19 and 129-146.

Yosida, K. (1978), Functional Analysis; 5th edition, Springer-Verlag, Berlin, Heidelberg, New York.

Vol. 157: Optimization and Operations Research. Proceedings 1977. Edited by R. Henn, B. Korte, and W. Oettli. VI, 270 pages. 1978.

Vol. 158: L. J. Cherene, Set Valued Dynamical Systems and Economic Flow. VIII, 83 pages. 1978.

Vol. 159: Some Aspects of the Foundations of General Equilibrium Theory: The Posthumous Papers of Peter J. Kalman. Edited by J. Green. VI, 167 pages. 1978.

Vol. 160: Integer Programming and Related Areas. A Classified Bibliography. Edited by D. Hausmann. XIV, 314 pages. 1978.

Vol. 161: M. J. Beckmann, Rank in Organizations. VIII, 164 pages. 1978.

Vol. 162: Recent Developments in Variable Structure Systems, Economics and Biology. Proceedings 1977. Edited by R. R. Mohler and A. Ruberti. VI, 326 pages. 1978.

Vol. 163: G. Fandel, Optimale Entscheidungen in Organisationen. VI, 143 Seiten. 1979.

Vol. 164: C. L. Hwang and A. S. M. Masud, Multiple Objective Decision Making – Methods and Applications. A State-of-the-Art Survey. XII, 351 pages. 1979.

Vol. 165: A. Maravall, Identification in Dynamic Shock-Error Models. VIII, 158 pages. 1979.

Vol. 166: R. Cuninghame-Green, Minimax Algebra. XI, 258 pages. 1979.

Vol. 167: M. Faber, Introduction to Modern Austrian Capital Theory. X, 196 pages. 1979.

Vol. 168: Convex Analysis and Mathematical Economics. Proceedings 1978. Edited by J. Kriens. V, 136 pages. 1979.

Vol. 169: A. Rapoport et al., Coalition Formation by Sophisticated Players. VII, 170 pages. 1979.

Vol. 170: A. E. Roth, Axiomatic Models of Bargaining. V, 121 pages. 1979.

Vol. 171: G. F. Newell, Approximate Behavior of Tandem Queues. XI, 410 pages. 1979.

Vol. 172: K. Neumann and U. Steinhardt, GERT Networks and the Time-Oriented Evaluation of Projects. 268 pages. 1979.

Vol. 173: S. Erlander, Optimal Spatial Interaction and the Gravity Model. VII, 107 pages. 1980.

Vol. 174: Extremal Methods and Systems Analysis. Edited by A. V. Fiacco and K. O. Kortanek. XI, 545 pages. 1980.

Vol. 175: S. K. Srinivasan and R. Subramanian, Probabilistic Analysis of Redundant Systems. VII, 356 pages. 1980.

Vol. 176: R. Färe, Laws of Diminishing Returns. VIII, 97 pages. 1980.

Vol. 177: Multiple Criteria Decision Making-Theory and Application. Proceedings, 1979. Edited by G. Fandel and T. Gal. XVI, 570 pages. 1980.

Vol. 178: M. N. Bhattacharyya, Comparison of Box-Jenkins and Bonn Monetary Model Prediction Performance. VII, 146 pages. 1980.

Vol. 179: Recent Results in Stochastic Programming. Proceedings, 1979. Edited by P. Kall and A. Prékopa. IX, 237 pages. 1980.

Vol. 180: J. F. Brotchie, J. W. Dickey and R. Sharpe, TOPAZ – General Planning Technique and its Applications at the Regional, Urban, and Facility Planning Levels. VII, 356 pages. 1980.

Vol. 181: H. D. Sherali and C. M. Shetty, Optimization with Disjunctive Constraints. VIII, 156 pages. 1980.

Vol. 182: J. Wolters, Stochastic Dynamic Properties of Linear Econometric Models. VIII, 154 pages. 1980.

Vol. 183: K. Schittkowski, Nonlinear Programming Codes. VIII, 242 pages. 1980.

Vol. 184: R. E. Burkard and U. Derigs, Assignment and Matching Problems: Solution Methods with FORTRAN-Programs. VIII, 148 pages. 1980.

Vol. 185: C. C. von Weizsäcker, Barriers to Entry. VI, 220 pages. 1980.

Vol. 186: Ch.-L. Hwang and K. Yoon, Multiple Attribute Decision Making – Methods and Applications. A State-of-the-Art-Survey. XI, 259 pages. 1981.

Vol. 187: W. Hock, K. Schittkowski, Test Examples for Nonlinear Programming Codes. V. 178 pages. 1981.

Vol. 188: D. Bös, Economic Theory of Public Enterprise. VII, 142 pages. 1981.

Vol. 189: A. P. Lüthi, Messung wirtschaftlicher Ungleichheit. IX, 287 pages. 1981.

Vol. 190: J. N. Morse, Organizations: Multiple Agents with Multiple Criteria. Proceedings, 1980. VI, 509 pages. 1981.

Vol. 191: H. R. Sneessens, Theory and Estimation of Macroeconomic Rationing Models. VII, 138 pages. 1981.

Vol. 192: H. J. Bierens: Robust Methods and Asymptotic Theory in Nonlinear Econometrics. IX, 198 pages. 1981.

Vol. 193: J. K. Sengupta, Optimal Decisions under Uncertainty. VII, 156 pages. 1981.

Vol. 194: R. W. Shephard, Cost and Production Functions. XI, 104 pages. 1981.

Vol. 195: H. W. Ursprung, Die elementare Katastrophentheorie. Eine Darstellung aus der Sicht der Ökonomie. VII, 332 pages. 1982.

Vol. 196: M. Nermuth, Information Structures in Economics. VIII, 236 pages. 1982.

Vol. 197: Integer Programming and Related Areas. A Classified Bibliography. 1978 – 1981. Edited by R. von Randow. XIV, 338 pages. 1982.

Vol. 198: P. Zweifel, Ein ökonomisches Modell des Arztverhaltens. XIX, 392 Seiten. 1982.

Vol. 199: Evaluating Mathematical Programming Techniques. Proceedings, 1981. Edited by J.M. Mulvey. XI, 379 pages. 1982.

Vol. 200: The Resource Sector in an Open Economy. Edited by H. Siebert. IX, 161 pages. 1984.

Vol. 201: P. M. C. de Boer, Price Effects in Input-Output-Relations: A Theoretical and Empirical Study for the Netherlands 1949–1967. X, 140 pages. 1982.

Vol. 202: U. Witt, J. Perske, SMS – A Program Package for Simulation and Gaming of Stochastic Market Processes and Learning Behavior. VII, 266 pages. 1982.

Vol. 203: Compilation of Input-Output Tables. Proceedings, 1981. Edited by J. V. Skolka. VII, 307 pages. 1982.

Vol. 204: K.C. Mosler, Entscheidungsregeln bei Risiko: Multivariate stochastische Dominanz. VII, 172 Seiten. 1982.

Vol. 205: R. Ramanathan, Introduction to the Theory of Economic Growth. IX, 347 pages. 1982.

Vol. 206: M.H. Karwan, V. Lotfi, J. Telgen, and S. Zionts, Redundancy in Mathematical Programming. VII, 286 pages. 1983.

Vol. 207: Y. Fujimori, Modern Analysis of Value Theory. X, 165 pages. 1982.

Vol. 208: Econometric Decision Models. Proceedings, 1981. Edited by J. Gruber. VI, 364 pages. 1983.

Vol. 209: Essays and Surveys on Multiple Criteria Decision Making. Proceedings, 1982. Edited by P. Hansen. VII, 441 pages. 1983.

Vol. 210: Technology, Organization and Economic Structure. Edited by R. Sato and M.J. Beckmann. VIII, 195 pages. 1983.

Vol. 211: P. van den Heuvel, The Stability of a Macroeconomic System with Quantity Constraints. VII, 169 pages. 1983.

Vol. 212: R. Sato and T. Nôno, Invariance Principles and the Structure of Technology. V, 94 pages. 1983.

Vol. 213: Aspiration Levels in Bargaining and Economic Decision Making. Proceedings, 1982. Edited by R. Tietz. VIII, 406 pages. 1983.

Vol. 214: M. Faber, H. Niemes und G. Stephan, Entropie, Umweltschutz und Rohstoffverbrauch. IX, 181 Seiten. 1983.

Vol. 215: Semi-Infinite Programming and Applications. Proceedings, 1981. Edited by A. V. Fiacco and K. O. Kortanek. XI, 322 pages. 1983.

Vol. 216: H. H. Müller, Fiscal Policies in a General Equilibrium Model with Persistent Unemployment. VI, 92 pages. 1983.

Vol. 217: Ch. Grootaert, The Relation Between Final Demand and Income Distribution. XIV, 105 pages. 1983.

Vol. 218: P. van Loon, A Dynamic Theory of the Firm: Production, Finance and Investment. VII, 191 pages. 1983.

Vol. 219: E. van Damme, Refinements of the Nash Equilibrium Concept. VI, 151 pages. 1983.

Vol. 220: M. Aoki, Notes on Economic Time Series Analysis: System Theoretic Perspectives. IX, 249 pages. 1983.

Vol. 221: S. Nakamura, An Inter-Industry Translog Model of Prices and Technical Change for the West German Economy. XIV, 290 pages. 1984.

Vol. 222: P. Meier, Energy Systems Analysis for Developing Countries. VI, 344 pages. 1984.

Vol. 223: W. Trockel, Market Demand. VIII, 205 pages. 1984.

Vol. 224: M. Kiy, Ein disaggregiertes Prognosesystem für die Bundesrepublik Deutschland. XVIII, 276 Seiten. 1984.

Vol. 225: T. R. von Ungern-Sternberg, Zur Analyse von Märkten mit unvollständiger Nachfragerinformation. IX, 125 Seiten. 1984

Vol. 226: Selected Topics in Operations Research and Mathematical Economics. Proceedings, 1983. Edited by G. Hammer and D. Pallaschke. IX, 478 pages. 1984.

Vol. 227: Risk and Capital. Proceedings, 1983. Edited by G. Bamberg and K. Spremann. VII, 306 pages. 1984.

Vol. 228: Nonlinear Models of Fluctuating Growth. Proceedings, 1983. Edited by R. M. Goodwin, M. Krüger and A. Vercelli. XVII, 277 pages. 1984.

Vol. 229: Interactive Decision Analysis. Proceedings, 1983. Edited by M. Grauer and A. P. Wierzbicki. VIII, 269 pages. 1984.

Vol. 230: Macro-Economic Planning with Conflicting Goals. Proceedings, 1982. Edited by M. Despontin, P. Nijkamp and J. Spronk. VI, 297 pages. 1984.

Vol. 231: G. F. Newell, The M/M/∞ Service System with Ranked Servers in Heavy Traffic. XI, 126 pages. 1984.

Vol. 232: L. Bauwens, Bayesian Full Information Analysis of Simultaneous Equation Models Using Integration by Monte Carlo. VI, 114 pages. 1984.

Vol. 233: G. Wagenhals, The World Copper Market. XI, 190 pages. 1984.

Vol. 234: B. C. Eaves, A Course in Triangulations for Solving Equations with Deformations. III, 302 pages. 1984.

Vol. 235: Stochastic Models in Reliability Theory. Proceedings, 1984. Edited by S. Osaki and Y. Hatoyama. VII, 212 pages. 1984.

Vol. 236: G. Gandolfo, P. C. Padoan, A Disequilibrium Model of Real and Financial Accumulation in an Open Economy. VI, 172 pages. 1984.

Vol. 237: Misspecification Analysis. Proceedings, 1983. Edited by T. K. Dijkstra. V, 129 pages. 1984.